PHAC

ARDENCY

ARDENCY

★

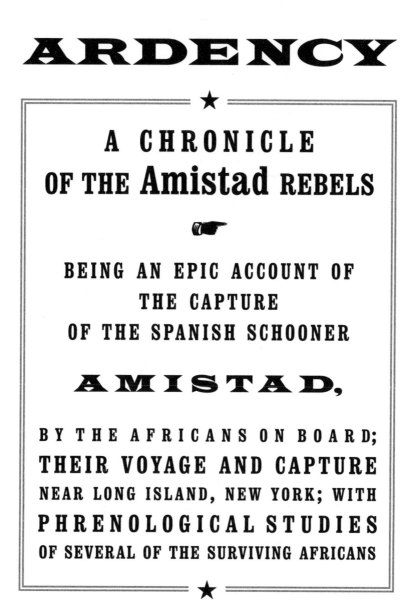

A CHRONICLE
OF THE Amistad REBELS

☞

BEING AN EPIC ACCOUNT OF
THE CAPTURE
OF THE SPANISH SCHOONER

AMISTAD,

BY THE AFRICANS ON BOARD;
THEIR VOYAGE AND CAPTURE
NEAR LONG ISLAND, NEW YORK; WITH
PHRENOLOGICAL STUDIES
OF SEVERAL OF THE SURVIVING AFRICANS

★

COMPILED FROM AUTHENTIC SOURCES BY

Kevin Lowell Young

Alfred A. Knopf   New York 2011

THIS IS A BORZOI BOOK
PUBLISHED BY ALFRED A. KNOPF

www.aaknopf.com

Knopf, Borzoi Books, and the colophon are registered trademarks
of Random House, Inc.

Library of Congress Cataloguing-in-Publication Data
Young, Kevin.
Ardency : a chronicle of the Amistad rebels / by Kevin Lowell Young.—
1st ed.
p.   cm.
ISBN 978-0-307-26764-1
1. Amistad (Schooner)—Poetry.   2. Slaves—United States—Poetry.
3. Slave insurrections—United States—Poetry.   4. Antislavery
movements—United States—Poetry.   I. Title.
PS3575.O798A85 2011
811'.54—dc22   2010030007

Jacket illustrations: From *A History of the Amistad Captives* . . .
by John Warner Barber, published by E. L. & J. W. Barber, 1840
Jacket design by Barbara de Wilde

Manufactured in the United States of America
First Edition

for Mama Annie

Painter, paint me a crazy jail, mad water-color cells.
Poet, how old is suffering? Write it in a yellow lead.

—Bob Kaufman,
Jail Poems

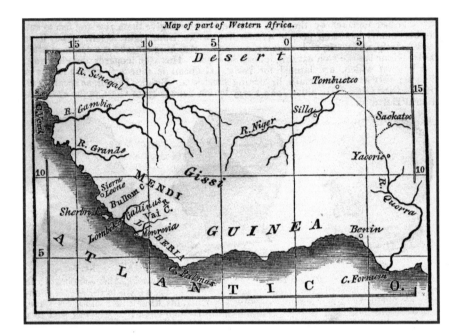

Map of part of Western Africa.

Preface.

In the summer of 1839, fifty-three Africans illegally sold in Havana mutinied on the schooner *Amistad* while being taken to Puerto Principe. The rebels, mostly men from the Mendi people of Sierra Leone, killed the captain and the cook but spared their masters to help steer toward the rising sun and Africa. For nearly two months, the would-be slaveowners rerouted by night until a navy brig captured the ship off the coast of Long Island. Authorities quickly threw the Africans in Connecticut jails while deciding either to return the men to their Spanish masters or award them as "salvage" to the U.S. sailors.

White abolitionists took up the case, converting the Mendi to Christianity and teaching them English in preparation for the trial. The book's first section, *Buzzard,* is in the voice of James Covey, twenty-year-old African interpreter for the imprisoned Mendi; *Correspondance* consists of the Mendi's letters and speeches from jail (and subsequent freedom); the third section, *Witness,* is a libretto spoken/sung by Cinque, leader of the rebellion.

★

Contents.

★

WITNESS.
A LIBRETTO

★

AFTER WORD;
or, THE MISSION & ITS FATE.

★

ARDENCY

★

Book-Keeping

Lomboko, Sierra Leone

1. Expenses Out.

Cost of *Tecora*, a 90-ton schooner.................... $ 3,700 00
Fitting out, sails, carpenter and cooper's bill........... 2,500 00
Provisions for crew and slaves 1,115 00
Wages advanced to 18 men before the mast 900 00
    "   "   to captain, mates, boatswain, steward, cook .. 440 00
200,000 cigars and 500 doubloons, cargo 10,900 00
Clearance and hush-money........................... 200 00

2. Expenses Home & In Havana.

Captain's head-money, at $8 a head................. $ 1,746 00
Mate's   ", Captain and Crew's wages 3,811 00
Government officers, at $8 per head................. 1,736 00
My commission on 217 slaves, expenses off 5,565 00
Consignee's commissions........................... 3,873 00
217 slave dresses, at $2 each....................... 434 00
Extra expenses of all kinds, say..................... 1,200 00

3. Returns.

Value of vessels at auction........................ $ 3,950 00
Proceeds of 217 slaves............................. 77,469 00

Total returns........................... $ 81,419 00
    "   expenses........................... 38,120 00

Net profit........................ $ 43,299 00

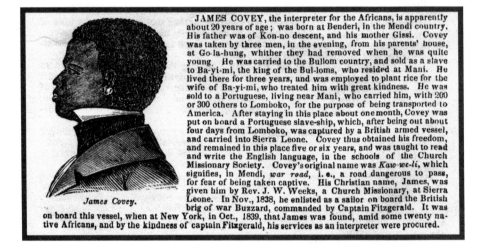

James Covey.

JAMES COVEY, the interpreter for the Africans, is apparently about 20 years of age; was born at Benderi, in the Mendi country, His father was of Kon-no descent, and his mother Gissi. Covey was taken by three men, in the evening, from his parents' house, at Go-la-hung, whither they had removed when he was quite young. He was carried to the Bullom country, and sold as a slave to Ba-yi-mi, the king of the Bul-loms, who resided at Mani. He lived there for three years, and was employed to plant rice for the wife of Ba-yi-mi, who treated him with great kindness. He was sold to a Portuguese, living near Mani, who carried him, with 200 or 300 others to Lomboko, for the purpose of being transported to America. After staying in this place about one month, Covey was put on board a Portuguese slave-ship, which, after being out about four days from Lomboko, was captured by a British armed vessel, and carried into Sierra Leone. Covey thus obtained his freedom, and remained in this place five or six years, and was taught to read and write the English language, in the schools of the Church Missionary Society. Covey's original name was *Kaw-we-li*, which signifies, in Mendi, *war road*, i. e., a road dangerous to pass, for fear of being taken captive. His Christian name, James, was given him by Rev. J. W. Weeks, a Church Missionary, at Sierra Leone. In Nov., 1838, he enlisted as a sailor on board the British brig of war Buzzard, commanded by Captain Fitzgerald. It was on board this vessel, when at New York, in Oct., 1839, that James was found, amid some twenty native Africans, and by the kindness of captain Fitzgerald, his services as an interpreter were procured.

BUZZARD.

And it came to pass at the end of forty days, that Noah opened the window of the ark which he had made:

And he sent forth a raven, which went forth to and fro, until the waters were dried up from the earth.

—*GENESIS 8:6–7*

Exodus

Gabriel, Escalastio, Desiderio,—in the seas beneath
the States, names new & Christian fell around you
like the lash. Before slavery, ten suns from water open
as a wound, you say you belonged to nothing
but home. Your back bore only spirit's teeth, scars
that meant manhood. Such rites of passage
protected little:—with in one moon you fared

no better than a slaver's shifting cargo of looking
glasses, olives. Out of boredom or freedom
of movement, the crew took a poker from under bitter
plaintains,—carved Captain's F into Cabin Boy's shoulder.
Parched as you were, would you have sipped the rum
& gunpowder smeared in that wound to make sure
it would brand? A few mad, swollen tongues caught

the saltwater Cabin Boy's good arm tossed. Was it
sanity drove cousin Fu-li to edge over the casket
of fresh water, lend it his own throat? Catching
him wet-lipped, Captain's men fed home
the whip:—even now you can hear his skin part,
can tell how much his body was water, how much
spine was book, just asking to be opened, read.

Covey

Hijacked on The War Road, my birth
name, each sun I walked in Africa
was a forgetting, each step a bird
song gone. Three men stole me:—a boy,
a bad dice roll, a debt traded for guns
& doubloons. I was to be like you, a slave
bowing to fields of sugar, a rebel raising

cane,—only a man-o-war turned my slaver
around, set me to work in Freetown
a servant. Anglicans christened me a small riot
of guineas,—half-Brit, half-bird, as Covey I served
Her Majesty's *Buzzard,* feeding off ships caught
& replanted, as I'd been. New World, eagle shore,
your abolitionists found me by counting:—one

versed in classics scoured the docks, parroted *eta,*
fili, wafura to every black face. Other hands laughed,—
to me those words held home, meant one, two, five,
free. From the wings I emerged:—step right up ladies
& Africans, feast your eyes on this Most Divine
Two-Tongue Man! Once *Kaw-we-li,* now Scavenger
of the Word, voice covering yours, I circle above.

Misericordia

Havana, Cuba

I hear you can buy a man
there easy as a name,—just check
the bottoms for red, telling
sores, examine teeth for words
like *runaway, no.* Your titles may
already bring you Spanish wine, or
quadroons in New Orleans gambling

halls, but Havana holds too many
Dons & men named for saints to take
such currency. Far off in the dark
continent, bars translate into goods,
a man's height in cotton, even kegs
of rum only fit for those negro backs
that taste the cat. This island speaks

only silver. One fifteen-dollar-a-head hand-
shake with Governor General can turn all
of Africa into *ladinos,* slaves born in Cuba
decades ago. The right signature
can make the youngest girl nineteen,
Christian, yours:—anything but white
or willing.

Cut-Up

Stop me if you've heard this one
before:—on a low, long, big black
boat, hunger follows you like sharks
along the Middle Passage. Oceans trail
blood & overboard brothers. You know
little about men who live at sea,
these white termites hoarding crumbs

for winters which never arrive. You
are the grasshopper men, locusts kept legless,
silent. Sold. Three days from Cuba, some body
steals over to Celestino, the rationing potato-
headed Cook, asks what does this routine of chains
mean? The griffin looks about for his master
& father, then leans closer to let you in

on some thing. Get this:—you'll be sliced, salted
& canned like laughter. His finger runs slow
across his neck, his body suddenly a tongue
even you can understand,—a joke on no body
but you. Here's a killer:—know why cannibals
don't eat clowns? Taste too funny. Your faces
never break, stay black as comedy.

Advent

You tell me you never answer to lion
or boy, tho the papers have called
you Jinqua, Singbe, Cinquez,
Sinner. You stay cold as ever
in your naked cell, refusing the grey
robes this Union wished you in.
I have seen enough heads read lately

to know yours will make even fools
famous, hands translating your body
in lectures, from podiums, where *such*
an African skull, well-formed, is seldom
to be seen—doubtless in other circumstances
an honor to his race. At sea, your masters
must have dreamt that crown would buy

them islands. They named you Joseph, step-
father to the Lord, slept & saw you bring Mary,
laboring, on a mule. How could they have known
your son across the sea whose name you confide
means God? They woke to the sounds of Xmas,
your cane knife opening the heads of lords
& mulattoes, like wisdom, molasses beneath stars.

Questioning

Who among you knew the Crew
split after seeing Captain's head
spill open? Who heard the lashings
come undone, or saw the gripe
unhooked, the lifeboat slip silent
over the side? While you knived
who saw the scar their cutter

made in water, slashing a wake
toward horizon, unseeable
shore? Who beheld the *Christ*
in your master's mouths as they watched
the night grow arms & strike? Did you
swab the sticky deck? Count casualties
like the black stars drown in?

Did you expect to meet ardency,
that wanting of wind? Who supposed
the stern would slow, your seizing
break, or guessed your masters,
while you slept, sailed for Providence?
And who let your dead launch
overboard, thrown like a voice?

Friendship

During the mutiny your Masters must have heard
Captain & his mulatto Messboy go down the way
such family should, fighting, each splash the black wax
sealing an envelope. *If it may please the court:*—tho hidden
behind hungry barrels, the traders still ordered that boy,
Antonio, to toss you bread & allegiance. You found
your owners scared as stowaways on that boat baptized

Friendship,—bound them in chains to give a taste
of a slave's thirst. For days the fools refused to believe
property could be so bold. It was as if the beds they'd made
love to, their favorite muskets, grew blue with waiting
& woke. Unvexed, they wrote strange script to hand
any ships chanced upon; you sunk such letters
of death, unswayed. You say you sent anchors over

the same way, hoping to cease your drift, then turn round
toward family. When your sunburnt enemy called the sea
too deep to stop, you dove down far as lungs & doubt allowed,
emerged only with handfuls of blind, angelic fish. Little choice
but spare the cretins to navigate by scorpion, twin:—let them
steer your fellowship of thieves, give them all the water
they please, free them from irons, only thing ever they shared.

Sightings

Having freed yourselves you wandered
like a Jew:—least that's how them Spaniards
saw you,—liable, bloodied, & without Christ
to save. By day, under watch, the Dons
steered sunward; nights they reversed west
& lied, left your inquisitions unmoored
no matter what your threat. You saw

horizon & hoped it home, landed to fill
your casks,—even then sensing this shore unsafe.
Nosing north, hungry, you ate from the hold
raisins & jaundice & wine. Some ate only angels,
died. Ships with names like lovers,—*Emmeline,*
Blossom—sighted & tried boarding your bandaged
ship, balked at the muskets, the black you brandished.

Rumors like scurvy spread:—up & down the coast,
Custom Collectors warn of your ghost ship,—
The Flying African. One night you spotted a halo,
corposant, ringing the broken mast. *San Elmo,*
the Spaniards whispered, crossing themselves double:—
a sign. After, in halcyon, yellowed, even you began
to believe,—your eyes grown wide & without white.

Washington

You harbored the ship like a criminal, stole
ashore hungry. Even eastward of Providence
reports had drifted of the strange spook
ship:—most thot you pirates, skin
the flag you never flew,—black covering skulls
& bones, crossed. When you signed for food,
dogs, folks drew water polite as blinds, then

called the pigs. Only Green, freelance captain,
would trade you goods. Wanted to turn you in
to gold,—stopped since you promised more
on board. While he haggled, the *Washington* found
your ship flagless, drunk with sea moss,—
covered in rent bags & one recent corpse.
Lieutenant added it up:—slaves & a fortune

in salvage. He sent you to the 3-ft. hold where Cinque
filled his belt with gold, leapt over the side. Sank. Swam out
of reach, an hour, while the brig searched. Drowning
the necklaces, surrendered himself. Reeled in, manacled,
Cinque pictures the necktie party the G-men got planned:—
I shall be hanged, I think, every day,—tongue flapping
a weather-beaten banner, pants full of freedom, soilt.

Experiment

Lieutenant swore you in on board
the *Experiment,* reading your Spanish names
like charges against you:—*Paschal, Santaria,*
Saturnio, Hipiloto. The right to remain
et cetera. Anything you say is in Mendi, mute
to them. I can only imagine & read what
the Spaniards you'd saved, sworn in, said:—

These chattel were born in Cuba, *bozales* bred
to be sold, not stolen. *Recollect*
who struck me but not the man saved me.
Had no wish to kill any of them, Lieutenant,
prevented them from killing each other. Asleep
I saw the whole thing. *Did not know how many*
days we were out. We kept no reckoning.

Soon you Mendi will holler with speech
of your own, saved like a dollar
or a soul,—*Can I get a witness?* Hands
on stacks of Bibles, you'll plea bargain
God. Leaping like faith,
O how you'll testify:—
Chariot, swing low, my, my.

Greeting

When we meet you grip my hand
as you drown,—say you never knew skin
even brown, could be so pale, polite.
You feel & fear you'll be turned in
side out. Jail's a far cry from those moons,
thirsting, you burnt up on ocean:—here
days dole sun stead of water.

Before stolen & set sail I never knew
any hue but the one you still wear,
that carbon some fools once tried
scrubbing off me at sea. I've since grown
used to being a shipman:—sea dog,
first mate, the chaste black sheep.
Shed more of me than you could

know. Boys, I been so long
upon the moors I've begun to feel
like one,—some poor painted Shake-
speare speaking tongues
not his own. If ever you read
my mind, or palm, you'd know this
shade hides a hot place, eclipsed.

Blackmarket

In the square vendors hawk your tale:—
the Africans are the lions of the day,
well-fed. Men fence colored etchings
of blacks opening the Captain's head.
In that market called flea, you fetch
a handsome fee,—ready to frame. Your names
hit The Bowery stage before you take

the stand, actors in cork putting on the mutiny
as musical:—*Zemba Cingues,* the savage
noble; *Cudjo, a deformed Dumb Negro;*
the fair damsel *Inez,* necessary, invented.
The Black Schooner rakes in thousands
while you wait captive as an audience
of assassins. In this market called free

you cost one shilling to see. The whole county flocks
to watch you at play, a flea circus somersetting
the prison Green. Warden claims the proceeds
for your bail & newspaper reviews of jail
go well:—*They crouch like tailors, teeth like stars*
in inky faces, black headlines blare. No one dares
how you still may be sold, stolen like a scene.

Tank

The abolitionists seek to school you
like fish. One cell over the girls weep,
share their grave-narrow bed. *This Jail*
Cinque wants to say, *is almost worst*
than the Drink. Solitary is one tank
without the think, his body
only evidence. The other men unwell,

sick as home. Days later, let out with sun,
they roll cartwheels in the yard
to tell they're alive. In the pen, still
fettered, Cinque stays under surveillance
as if water,—the kind that gathers
on the brain. He's going down a third time
but no one sees him wave.

Who wouldn't want to join Davey Jones,—
he musta been black with a name
like that—little wonder he went overboard,
locked up drum-tight. Still, it hushed us all
when Foone followed suit:—a strong swimmer
by all accounts, he waded out with his weighted-
down heart, never saw our shore again.

Eyetooth

Seems like every day another curator
or ivied student comes to draw
the captives like blood, render them
in profile,—varnished, unreadable coins.
Today the leech doctors decide Konoma
isn't cannibal, that his bucked out
& filed teeth crave nothing besides

English. New Haven dailies report:—
one said to belong to the man-eating
Caronmanche tribe denies, as well
as we could understand, ever tasting
human flesh. His quick tongue, not Mendi,
confuses even me. He points out diamonds
tattooed to his fore head, makes me know

he keeps many names. I exchange that
a specialist can pull his jaw, will rein
his incisors for nothing. *There certainly is*
far more destructiveness in the look
of his protruding mouth than caught up
in his brain. The one we call Nazha-u-lu
smiles, refuses, turns the other tooth.

Findings

Before bed I read out the book that bares
news of Cinque's skull:—*The captive appears*
to have twenty-six years of age, a temperament
sanguine and bilious; the bilious predominates.
His head is over two feet from nose's root
to the Meatus Auditorius, a hand's width
at destructiveness. Fletcher, phrenologist

to the Queen, hunts Cinque's head like lice,
finding *his faculties hope, esteem, firmness,—*
very large. No shrink asks me to bow like prayer
to search me for genus,—my smart box hidden by hair
& hand kerchief. *Caution, combat, adhesion, order,*
philoprogenitiveness, individuality, eventuality, causality,
secrecy, language,—average. Better to be read badly

or remain undiscovered? *Veneration, form, wonder,*
comparison, inhabitiveness, benevolence,—large. I fear,
unlike Fletcher, I may never touch genius or learn
what men's heads hold. *Acquisition, imitation,*
ideals, mirth, number, size, weight, time, tune,
color,—moderate, small. Could this be my fate,
my invisible art, to translate an opaque race?

Easter

Father:—I regret not having
sent word sooner. Here the Mendi
have begun to crack my knuckles
in greeting, to trust my words
like birds settling back on the branch
of my tongue,—forked, divining.
They write & learn things

quick as death. This makes me good,
reminds me how you adopted
& raised me like the dead, learning me
to say *pardon* to every passing
soul. Still, my interpretations loom less
necessary daily. Every letter they send
a sail, drawing home near.

I fear most the waking, watching them
leave to discover their own sun
& country. My sir, must we stand
to bring up what deserts us? Too soon,
it seems, I must close. May my words
reach you in manners I never can, crossing
boundless blue between. Yours, I remain,—

Maroon

How I hated you, dear Antonio, when you sang
of good treatment by the same masters
who'd branded you. When before God & every
one you swore the Mendi craved white men's
brains. I think we all shook our skulls
as the court swallowed that shuffle & jive:—
here comes the judge, here go the usual

suspects. Called to the stand, I felt so African
& pure, knowing something of a homeland,
some former name. All you had, Cabin Boy,
was your broken Spanglish. I know now
you were leaving, had planned
escape for days. How I picture you today,—
the laughing buffalo boy, trading tricks & skins

with the Indians. Brer Antonio with the rabbit
smile, not one rebel or pale prosecutor
saw you disappear among hounded hills. No body
watched you unhook yourself, sail quietly off. How
I envy the manner you turned up missing, a tooth
darkening, then fallen away. How our tongues
change, exposed, explore that space you've made.

Broadway

At Broadway Tabernacle the abolitionists charge
half-dollar a head to view your Mendi zoo.
After the slideshow of Sierra Leone, they hold
spelling bees to show how far you've come.
I wish for a word I could become. If just one letter
would shift, *worship* turning *warship* . . . But little
Kale spells it right:—*Bless-ed are the pure at heart.*

Freed, you've grown used to belting hymns
at the drop of a hat, then passing the plate
about. Tonight will rake in enough
to buy your craft & ship your selves home.
I want to join your crew
like a church, catch the red-eye to Africa,—
or at least Death's ferry, stowing away

to heaven. Let out the pews you Mendi jig,—
a crowd gathers, gives—& the men stoop
for change to buy some thing beside soft
shoes. The high-collar Committee has you return
the cash, prefers sideshows only under steeples,
pomp under certain circumstance. No one asks
after me,—still I dance, secret, with in my skin.

Calling

Mine is the most unseen art:—I make
others make sense. I take
your foreign tongue,—the one
I once was part—& turn it
to polite. I read minds better
than those shrinks the Committee called
in,—wonder whether, on your Mission

in Mendi, shall you think of me? Or just
Jesus? My calling is to vanish, finish
the thoughts others don't know
they own. My sea legs,—bow,
winded—wish to drift like wood.
Mines be the sailor's need:—to see
the world through a spyglass, find

myself awake in a country stranger
than skin. Never to be owned, or owe
any one a thing. I am a dream
the Lord, lonely,
had of earth,—have only
His mirror's desire:—to see
myself translated, made echo, you.

Soundings

We set course as if a meal, aim
like prayer home. Our ship
a barque name of *Gentleman,*—
what we's become—booked
& bobbing the harbor. I board
unbelieving,—fearing Customs
will hone in & call us bucaniers,

book us for stealing ourselves.
Instead, the men sing God
by the monkey gaff. No flags fly. Christ,
our new Pilot, provides. Sent to set
the mission up, Steele hits his Good
Book with a thump. Says we
been saved. The boat rocks.

The men shed clothes & English
soon as we set foot on solid ground.
See shore. See Mendi run. Our skin
again ours, blackens, a taut drum.
Either loud or without
a sound, each passenger like a pigeon
takes wing,—hunted, homing.

Revelations

Mother:—time you get this I shall have flown
these States all together. The Committee raised
money like Jesus or bread,—I convinced myself
& the anti-slavers I had nothing left here
but second-hand words. Mother, some days
I wonder about the one who isn't you,
the one who birthed me & calls me dead

or stolen. I hope tonight to smuggle myself
home the same way. Mother, in all my nightly
horses my feet finally touch ground
then my lips,—looking up, the men scatter,
leaving shadows where bodies stood
one breath before. Home for them is whatever
they become, tho my arms fail wings.

Mother, when this letter arrives I hope
to have it told you already, your face & the trees
reminding us that wind drags words
far behind bodies. My words the barnacles
clutching ship's wood, helpless, helping
themselves. Wait & they will spring
geese from my mouth. In Christ & haste,—

3 feet 3 in. high

[The above engraving shows the position as described by Cingue and his companions, in which they were confined on board the slaver, during their passage from Africa. The space between the decks represented in the engraving is three feet three inches, being an actual measurement from a slave vessel. The space in the vessel that brought the Amistad captives to Havana was, according to their statement, somewhat larger, being about four feet between the decks.]

CORRESPONDANCE.

Canst thou draw out leviathan with an hook?
or his tongue with a cord *which* thou lettest down?

Canst thou put an hook into his nose? or bore his
jaw through with a thorn?

Will he make many supplications unto thee? will he
speak soft *words* unto thee?

Will he make a covenant with thee? wilt thou take
him for a servant for ever?

Wilt thou play with him as *with* a bird? or wilt thou
bind him for thy maidens?

Shall the companions make a banquet of him? shall
they part him among the merchants?

Canst thou fill his skin with barbed irons? Or his
head with fish spears?

Lay thine hand upon him, remember the battle,
do no more.

—JOB 41:1–8

New England Primer

Apricots
In Adam's *Fall*
We Sinnéd All.

Betrayal
Thy Life to Mend
This Book *Attend.*

Capture
The Cat *doth play*
And after Slay.

Darkness
A Dog *will bite*
A thief at night.

Eggshell
An Eagle's *flight*
Is out of sight.

Forgetting
The Idle Fool *is*
Whipt at School.

Westville

dear Sir   Mr tappan

I want tell you Some thing   I going to write you a letter   I will write you
a few lines my friend   I am began to write you a letter   I bless you because
I love you   I want pray for you every night and every morning and evening
and I want love you too much   I will write letter for you from that time
Jesus began to preach and say repent   for the kingdom of heaven is at
hand   My Dear friend I thanks you a plenty because you Send me letter
and I thank you for it and I want pray for you every evening and every
night and every morning by day and by night and his always

Mr Tappin   Love us   pray our father who art in heaven hallowed be
I want to tell you Some thing   I have no hat   Dear Sir I write you if you
please and so kind I please you   that I please you Let me have A hat to
cover my head   that I please you dear friend I tell you Some thing   I please
you that you let me have A bible   my friend I want you give me A hat
and I thank you a plenty   and I have no bible and hat both

my friend I give you good loves   I believe you are my friend   my Sir I
want you tell your friends my good loves   I want love all teachers who
teach me and all my people good things about Jesus Christ God and heaven
and every things   I bless them that teach me good   I pray for them I want
write some   your name   thy kingdom come thy will be done in earth as it is
in heaven give us this day our daily bread and forgive us our debts as we
forgive forgive our debtors for thine is the kingdom and the power
and the glory for ever Amen   O Lord   my friend I write this paper to you
because I love you too much   my Sir   I want to tell you Some thing

When we in havana vessel we have no water to drink   when we eat rice
white man no give us to drink   when Sun Set white men give us little water
when we in havana vessel white men give rice to all who no eat   fast he
take whip you   a plenty of them died and havana men take them put in
water   I try to write letter of paper for Mr you   and Jesus said unto him No
man having put his hand to the plough and looking back is fit for
the kingdom of God   my friend I am Stop writing your letter   Gone To you
a letter   my name Kale   I am your friend   I give you this letter

Speech

having English now
I hope to tell you what
it meant to hear your
words it was a river
slowly icing over it was
rain falling into water
was the night following
rain into water a father
crocodile waking early
to eat his children it
became the memory

of a gourd at my lips
the salt surrounding
the ship so white
& useless it was a thirst
a message thrown over
board a bottle a sudden
ash upon our skin our
tongues grown dark
& unavoidable as bay
leaves I thank you gentle
men for lending us yours

New Haven

Dear Friend Mr. Adams,

I want to write a letter to you because you love Mendi
people and you talk to the grand court. We want to tell you
one thing; stranger say we born in Havana, he tell lie. We stay
in Havana 10 days and 10 nights, we stay no more. We all
born in Mendi. Mendi people been in Merica 17 moons. We
write every day; we write plenty letters; we read most all
ways; we read Matthew, and Mark, and Luke, and John,
and plenty of little books. We love books very much.

We want you to ask the court what we have done wrong. What
for Mericans keep us in prison? Some men say Mendi people
very happy because they laugh and have plenty to eat. No body
give Mendi people any these things. Mr. Judge come with bars
and sentences and Mendi people all look sorry. O we can't tell
how sorry. Some people say Mendi people no got souls, white
men afraid of Mendi people. Then we laugh. Why we feel bad
we got no souls?

Dear friend Mr. Quincy, you have children, you have
friends, you love them, you feel very sorry if Mendi people come
and carry them all to Africa. When Mr. Jailer came hear with
chains he put on some hands and he whip them to hard, he no feel
a shame. We afraid for Merica people because Merica people say
we make you free. If Merica people give us free we glad, if they no
give us free we sorry; sorry for Mendi people little; sorry for Merica
people great deal because God punish liars.

We want you to tell the court that Mendi people no want to go back
to New Havana, we no want to be killed. Dear friend you tell our Judges
let us free. Dear friend we want to know how we feel. Mendi people
think, think, think. No body know what we think. We think we know God

punish us if we have lie. We never tell lie; we fill truth. What for
Mendi people afraid? Because they got souls.

Cook says he kill, he eat Mendi people;
we afraid; we kill cook. Then captain kill one man with knife, and lick
Mendi people plenty. We never kill captain, he kill us. If court ask who
brought Mendi people to Merica? We bring ourselves. We hold
the rudder. All we want is make us free.

This from my hand,
Kin-na

Testimony

You call us rebels   we were spoons
in that ship for so long   the wood
dark, drowned as the men who
made it from song   sold on land
like ships   like us   christened
out of water   You call us rebels
we were thrown with schools of fish
in the stomach of that ship   we slept
with the dead   which is not at all
You call us rebels   one day we took
the wheel from men with eyes of
water   we turned the ship towards
the rising sun   let the wind grace
our backs   that night we slept like
anchors   that night the sailors
turned us towards a Newborn
England   in dawn we saw blesséd
land   then felt the sun's heat
betraying our backs   too late
we saw the sunless men   their navy
racing   to rescue us into chains
now we know the edge of setting
sun   where only the dead are free
to come and go as you please

Farmington

Dear Friend
Mr. L. Tappan

I embrace this opportunity of writing a few
lines to you to inform you that I am well & when
this come to your hand & I hope that it may find you
in good health   & yesterday our Judge set little
girls free & we are thankful   & girls have free
now   & I hope great God will bless you & keep
those who want hurt you

& Tuesday night I wish & thank you very much
because you make us free & Mr Adams he made us
free & Menda people thank you very much   I pray for you
& I am sorry to hear your Children have sick   I hope God
to make them get well   & I hope great God will bless you
& be my dear benefactory

& I will pray for you when I go to bed and when
you rise in the morning & when you go to bed   & what
we want you to do will you do it   & I call you Dear Father
because you so kind to poor Menda   & I wish pray to great
God to send us to our home   he sent his Son to the world
to save us from going down to held

all men have some work to do   & suppose you must
let us go home & tell them about you   jesus said unto him
foxes have holes & birds of the air have nests but the son
of man hath not where to lay his head   My friend I want
you to carry us into Sierra Leone

& this from your friend
Banna

Gospel

It's me It's me
It's me O Lord
Standing in
the need of prayer

It's me It's me
It's me O Lord
Standing in
the needle prayer

Not my brother
Not my sister
but it's me O Lord
Standing in
the eve of prayer

Not my mother
Not my father
but it's me O Lord
Standing in
the eaten prayer

Con.

President Tyler:

You have done a great deal
for us. Now we want to go home, very
much, very soon. When we get to Sierra
Leone, we get home, we find a good
place for our teachers, then tell enemies
and friends come see them. We want
plenty of calicoes, not cut, for men's coats,
pantaloons. For we think we wear Merica
dress as long as we live. We want plenty
to give our friends and have them give
us elephant teeth, camwood, palm
oil, and other things to send you
to Merica. We will take good care
of our teachers. We will not
leave them.
        When we are in Mendi we never
hear of such a thing as men taken away
and carried to Cuba, and then return back
home again. The first thing we tell
them will be that great wind bring
us back. We tell them all about
Merica. We tell them about God
and how Jesus Christ, his only beloved
Son, came to down to die for us, and we
tell them to believe, for these your sons
were lost before now. We want you
to give your children to us, give
to the teachers to teach them
to pray, and not to pray to any
thing but God.

Some wicked people here
laugh at all our Committee
for spending so much on Mendi
people. They say we are like dogs
without any home. But if you will
send us home, you will see whether we
be dogs or not. O please let us go
to the Africa. We want to see no more
snow. We no say this place no good,
but we afraid of cold. Cold catch us all
the time.

With becoming respect &c.,

MR. CINQUE

Scripture

The schooner to hell is a cold long
ride, the wind a doctor rapping

your chest, touching your hair
marking it *unusual, warm lamb's*

wool. You shall travel
west, heading into that bed

the sun drops into after another day
of waking cousins caught in chill

oceans. Once there, you won't
find drums, hell has no percussion

to speak of,—here you can only beat
your belly, its sound growing

thin, thinner. Hell is all
coughs, professors saying *bless*

you and writing it down,—you'll
learn the line, the cut, promises

of freedom. You'll wait, counting
voices, sleep, Bible verses. Let all

the hearers of God's word row
forth, bowing, into the world.

Boston, Mass.

November 8, 1841

To the Hon. John Quincy Adams:

Most Respected Sir,—the Mendi people will never
forget your defence of their rights before the Great

Court of Washington. They feel that they owe
to you, in a large measure, their delivery from evil

hands. They will pray for you as long as you live
Mr. Adams. They never forget you. We are about

to go home, to Africa, we reach Mendi very quick,
then tell the people of your kindness. Good

missionary will go with us. We will take black
Bibles in our mouths,—it has been a precious book

in prison, in writing you, in fire, and we love
to read it now we are free. Mr. Adams we want

to make you a present of a beautiful
Bible. Please accept it, and when you look

at it, remember your grateful clients. We read
in this holy book:—*If it had not been the Lord*

upon our backs when men rose up against us,
then they had swallowed us up quick. Blessèd

be the Lord, who has not given us a prey
to their teeth. Our soul is escaped as a bird

out of the fowler's snare,—the snare is broken
and we soar into the gate and airs of Heaven.

For the Mendi people,
Cinque
Kinna
Kale

Sermon

Heaven has to be this
hot shady place where
folks drink from sky

where we *Preach*
now flood with the hint
of rain where no one

crosses *All right* rivers
of hounds & the thirsty
sip from wells full

of flowers & fallen men
where no man owns
any thing or you or your

mama where some *Praise*
the Lord people starve some
don't but no body thins no

one else where it ain't all gold
harps but nothing swims
a slave *A-men*

Gentleman

at sea, near Sierra Leone

January 13, 1842

Dearest Tappan—this Captain good—
no touch Mende people. We have seen
great water—no danger fell upon
us. I tell you to make letters
for those who no touch us. All
Mende people glad for white men

you give to go with us. Mister
Steele—he left ship to find place. He stop
in Tucker's town—who drink rum all
the time—who is a drunkard. Who like
money better than his own soul. He
tell us the ground costs six hundred

bars—Steele would not give so much.
All the rest of Mende left ship to find
their parents. I think that they will
come again. If they no come, I think
God will punish them forever—one
day. You see we are ten now to stay

behind Steele, and three girls. We will
work wood, we will farm and cut
for him every day. You no feel
bad for that—dear friend—some
Mende men will take care
of your mission. Soon I catch

Sierra Leone—my country—make
home—and take care of white
man. Oh, dear Mister Tappan
how I feel for these wondrous
things! I cannot write so true
because the ship rolls. Pray—

Jesus will hear you—if I never
see you in this world—send word
from the next and the new—

GEORGE BROWN (FU-LI)

Toast

Sad indeed, sad in mind, eighteen
forty-two was a hell of a time when
the news reached a free sea town:—
the barque *Gentleman* was going down.

They tell me on board was a fella named Shine,
so damn dark he changed the world's mind.
The Captain and the Cook began exchanging
words until that ship hit the first iceberg.

Up came Shine from down below, saying,
"Cap'n, Cap'n, don't you know they's
four feet of water on the galley floor." Captain
looked Shine straight dead in the eye

didn't ask how, didn't care why. He said,
"Go on south and start stacking sacks,—
I got all you darkies to keep that water back."
The Cook and the Captain kept exchanging words

until this *Gentleman* hit the next iceberg.
Up came Shine from down below, sayin,
"Cap'n, Cap'n, can't work no more
with forty feet of water on the galley floor."

Captain said, "Shine, Shine, that can't be a fact,
I've got you bucks to keep that water back."
Shine went back below, began to think.
"This big motherfucker's bound to sink!

"There's sharks in the ocean, sharks in the sea
no way this Great White's gonna bullshit me.
I'd rather be in that drink going round
than on this mother going sure down."

Shine hit the water and began to swim
a million millionaires staring at him.
Shine took a single overhand stroke,
sailed five miles from that sinkin boat.

Big Money Captain came on deck, pants
all stiff with his wet book of checks,
singing, "Shine, Shine, if you save poor me
I'll make you as rich as a blackman can be."

Shine plied, "You hate my color, you down on my race,
get your ass overboard and loan a shark a taste."
Shine started stroking, stroking and yellin,
kicking up water like a showboat propeller.

Big Captain's Wife came on deck, white
gold and ivory all round her neck,
singing, "Shine, Shine if you save my life
I'll be your faithful wedded wife."

Shine plied, "I know you are fine and that
is true, but women back home make an ass
of you. Ass on land, ass at sea, get your
ass overboard and swim like me."

Big Preacherman came on deck,
Bible in one hand, cross round his neck,
singing, "Shine, Shine if you save poor me
I'll make you as saved as any blackman can be."

Shine plied, "Lords in the ocean, Baptists in the sea,
Get your ass overboard and swim like me."
Shine bowed his head and began to swim, all
Those millionaires still tracking him.

Big Daughter of the Revolution came on deck,
drawers round her knees, dress round her neck,

singing, "Shine, Shine if you save poor me
I'll give you more ass than a blackman can be."

Shine plied, "White girl, you must think I'm
blind! First I've got to save this black behind.
Ass on land, ass at sea, ass on land
is enough for me."

Big Abolitionists came on deck, pens
in their hands, chains behind their backs,
singing, "Shine, Shine if you save poor we
We'll make thee more free than a blackman can be."

Shine plied, "Some thing bout you folks I'll never
understand,—you wouldn't give me that when we both
shared land." Before the last words fell from his lips
Shine soared fifty leagues from that drowning ship.

Big White Shark came up from the bottom of the sea
singing, "Look what Godalmighty gave to me!
Shine, Shine, you're stroking fine, miss
one stroke, your ass is mine."

Shine bowed his neck and showed his ass,—
"Get out the way and let a big fish pass."
Shine kept stroking till he hit shore, then he
stroked and stroked and stroked some more.

By the time the *Gentleman* was almost
sunk, Shine reeled on shore, off his ass
drunk, dancing and spreading it all a-round
how this old fucker had just gone down.

"Shine," everyone said, "Shine how you know?"
I left that mother sinkin million heartbeats ago.

Freetown

Sierra Leone, West Africa

October 6th, 1842

MY DEAR SIR—Pray excuse
me, for I have never spoken
to you, nor had the privilege
of seeing you. I am your perfect

stranger, but I feel thankful
for what Committee has done
for the Mendians. Though
I am not of the same

tribe, we are all Africans.
As for my part, I am
a native of A-ku, stolen
from my parents and sold

as a slave. It pleased
the Lord to send English
men to deliver us
from chains. In 1829, they gave

me to the government
school as servant boy
to the Manager
of this colony. I never

had an opportunity
to attend the house
of God until late in 1837
when the Lord convinced

me of my sins, blessed
my soul. I always thought

I was doing very well, but
behold I was a very ignorant

boy. I never knew this
until Mr. Steele removed
here. One forenoon
I sat under his

sermon. I said to myself
I do not want his gospel
to end. I kept very near
to him. Bye and bye

one Sunday I went
to chapel. From that
glorious meeting I began
to feel I had nothing

but a miserable soul.
I said to myself what
shall I do to escape
all this? In June

he commenced Temperance.
This thing I was quite
a stranger to—I never
heard such a society

in the world. I went
and signed the pledge.
From that time, I have
had nothing to do

with anything that is
intoxicating. I pray
God that a double
portion of his berry

blood may rest upon
your throat this day—
may his blessing attend
all your faithful

labors. Please
excuse this your humble
servant in these
the bonds of God.

W. HENRY GRAHAM

No. 1.

(1.)Sing-gbe,[**Cin-gue,**](generally spelt *Cinquez*)was born in Ma-ni, in Dzho-poa, *i. e.* in *the open land*, in the Men-di country. The distance from Mani to Lomboko, he says, is ten suns, or days. His mother is dead, and he lived with his father. He has a wife and three children, one son and two daughters. His son's name is *Ge-waw*, (God.) His king, Ka-lum-bo, lived at Kaw-men-di, a large town in the Mendi country. He is a planter of rice, and never owned or sold slaves. He was seized by four men, when traveling in the road, and his right hand tied to his neck. Ma-ya-gi-la-lo sold him to Ba-ma-dzha, son of Shaka, king of Gen-du-ma, in the Vai country. Bamadzha carried him to Lomboko and sold him to a Spaniard. He was with Mayagilalo three nights; with Bamadzha one month, and at Lomboko two months. He had heard of Pedro Blanco, who lived at Te-i-lu, near Lomboko.*

WITNESS.

☞ *A LIBRETTO*

I was not in safety, neither had I rest, neither was
I quiet; yet trouble came.

—JOB 3:26

I. Processional.

I was in the wilderness
the wild——

Ah was without the Lawd

I was asleep
or walked in dream
—it matters not—

when the men set
upon me—seiz'd—
sacked—

First I thot them
missionaries

learned I then
I was debt——

they were to take me far
from this—my only—home—

far from Sierra Leone
the mountain lion—my land—

Had I heard
of such a thing—*yes*—

We have many
devil who the night prowl——

But I knew not
of Hell:—

ferried across
to this cold
cold place,—

Knew not the Word,—

only us joined
brothered—in the hold——

was stank

was shat & a sea
of vomit——

The sick were not
set free
their Misery:—

was the wails
that 'most swallowed
me up—

all night the cries
of chillens,—

Many thousand gone
Many million lost,—

Ah knew not the Lawd—

None here
—below—in the berth—
I knew

yet all were of me
mine

Each tongue I understood:—

   Death
in the mouth——
death in the loin
& lung, in the breath
death,—

      Many stomachs
      spake with one voice,—

         Many many done gone——

   We begged our old
   gods

Our cries on deaf
ears fell

like the lash,—ash—

   Young & old,
   even the dead were not spared
   —none buried—

We were not let light:——

   We saw no ground
   for many moons

      Once was lost
      but now—I'se found—

How many the sea
swallow'd—I could
not say—see—

Ah was not of the Lawd

upon our throat
water was trickled
—wrung—from a rag

    the rice our people
for generations
grew—forced
down our gullet—

      it mattered not——

our lips cracked
like a rock
struck & made to weep—

      Ah was not long
      without the Lawd

and lo, up-on the sea——

Choir (Evening)

Sang.
Sang against the storm

and through.
Sang the warm rain.

And the cold.
And our voices growing

hoarse with wind.

No talk
of heaven—

though we learnt that
too up-on the ocean.

Blood that isn't kin.

No supper
to sang for. Nothing

but ration. Heaven
ain't the end—

Heaven begins
the steady lifting.

Things I don't have
no word for——

bones lining the ocean floor.

Hush, child.
The rain. My voice all

I carried.

★

II. Passages.

¶ A man shall eat good by the fruit of his mouth: but the soul of the transgressors shall eat violence.

—Proverbs 13: 2

Homily

I have been wandered wild over this world
not by choice:—force

found me in my village,
or in sleep, walking the low
lovely huts, my children's voices——

I have been called
from these things to this
world,—never was new

to me—the birds still
sing—the sun—my heart
in the cage of my chest

crying out like a parrot.
I learnt their talk. Caught
and given no more sky, I fought

as any would. The wood
of the slaver against my back
became my back—the bow

and stern of it, the slow
slow sailing.
                    Who recalls, if at the prow,
I met a mermaid's welcome?

My wife far and *frozen*—a word
I would not have known
if not for you—who would

guess of mist made
cold? Tho I had heard tell
of Death, I never knew

its stillness could, in cold, have no smell.

★

The living thing I loved. Stood
and breathed in. Breathed.
They came, the breaths, often

in home's hills,—they came not at all
in that hold, crouched cramped
cattled—Death came for us

among the moaning the rattling,
the men ghosting, wails
of the women, our children quiet . . .

No child should ever say
such quiet. Be loud!
Death there like a sweetness:—

a hum, a milk song each child
grew hush for.

★

We spoke with hands we did
not have. Our arms not ours,—
to bear and to bury was all

they'd become. The young ones,—
who would no longer
grow one day older—the waves part for

and the squid find. The arms
of the deep—the many
many hands—rock them

into sleep.

★

All night we sang
not of Death,—the cut
down tree—but of that

fruit you call *free*.

Petition

Two trains a day
ran—the way
we wanted to

    trapped in them
    barracoons—

from the cars merchants
leaned & bought
bodies—bucks—

    Let the buyer
    beware

Some of the wares
we—was sick—

Some too well
& would split
like a skull

        I been down
        I been down
        Been down in-to
        the sea

This Cuba they call it—
This market in men—

        I been
        I been babtized
        in Je-sus' name

Been down in the sea

Paper renames us

We are traded
& in the night
smuggled down

    to all the ships
    that sail for other
shores

We are
by definition dead,—

    unable to speak
    or sing—of *sin*—

We march
toward the sea

    shackled—
shackled—
    shackled—

shuffled many miles

    Oh won't dem
    mourners rise
    an' tell

We board her
broad back—*La Amistad*—
what will bear us
to Porte Principé—

    Been down in the sea

            Two trains
a day ran, two trains
a day—

        O how long was Jonah
        in the bowels
        of the whale:—

            For three whole days
            and nights he sailed

bound—
we are—for Hell—

        Halleloo——

Libations

Master, I have meant
no ill—

have slain
one of Your sons—some—

*One day when I was
lost,—*

have let
blood, like a leech,
a doctor,—impatient—
left men

to die:—

*I know it was the blood
for me (the blood for me)*

from my palm
pulled the nail

tore off our chain:—

No longer tied
each to each
other

No longer
brothers—
keepers—

the first blow
from my hand fell

                pierced
        by the blood
              the body,—

                  We were the best
                  of thieves—*blest*—

                  from my side spilled
                  my followers

        Forgive:—

              felled the Captain
        his colored cook
        like Paradise—jawbone
        of an ass—

        Forgive them Father
        for they know not

        Forgive me Father for

        Am I not a brother
              kept near?

        We raised up
              our arms
        like a cup

                  and so drank:——

Mass (Ordinary)

Credo.

I believe the body——

The body of beggars
& saints—are same—

I have seen
—by my hand—
a man bleed

& be not buried
except by sea——

I believe

I believe in the sound
the soul makes

No rites we were
offered at all—just
dumped—dogs—

O how they despaired us—

Thot us scraps—scars——

I believe in skin

I believe in its span
& its shrill
sanctuary——

Gloria.

I was in the storm
without a way—
      I was shown:—

Three days up-on the sea
and sent up a wish
—*Free-dom*

      free-dom from
      this toil

The sea shuddering
—a man
shouldering some great wait

      bearing him down,—

The flock
of birds in my chest
lifted up—
      as one——

      We shored
      ourselves

Like a clock
we bore arms
      & struck:—

Sanctus.

And so sought
shelter—from ourselves—
the storm

Our masters lashed
to the mast
—the sirens—

A sanctuary
we could not steer

We were not starwise

    And so
    I sent us—I thot—into sun—

Agnus Dei.

And somehow
by the dark
they blamed us for

    our masters made west
    without compass

Many us died from thirst
or drinking
of medicine—men——

    We kept no log,
only water——

    We landed this Is-
land Merica,—

It is by sea
surrounded
and by fury—the harpies

    at us tear——

    We landed this Sound
It is sand

beneath our feet
    It gives——

Testament

Exiled ghosts
headed toward Jerusalem & sun

Two months at sea without jibs or top
sails pale as a judge's wig

The charges against us false as teeth

By day their skin a white flag
of truce—each night the Spaniards

turning to fight
what light we steered by

They thot us without mothers
or tongues—till ours

swole up, turning rudders—
thick—with thirst—

Chantey

We migrate—
eliminate

the middle
passage man—

Soon we'll sell
ourselves

to crowds—free—
so's they'll send us

to Sierra Leone—
home—

Less go—

★

For now, risen
up like that *nigger*

Lucifer,
we rule our roost—

★

We bend toward
sunrise—the seas

are kind
till wind

grows against us—
We send

into it, weighting

what the sailors name
ardency—

★

Land. We been
headed for

sunrise so long
I forgot home

had a dusk—
had what these whites

call West—
the past—what was—

a *sun*—fallen—

★

Heaven's
a hog

we haven't eaten
—*yet*—

Doxology

We sailed awash
with treason and sun

which beat down
up-on us,—as once
our masters had

This was long
before we knew our sole
Master—Lawd—You

Before we
knew Thee:—

We was lost Lawd
upon that great sea

what you call weeks
went by—water—brine—
our thirst grew strong

our insides scurvy soft,—

Still I sent
the Spaniards mercy:—my share
of water touched their lips
—their trembled teeth—

before any wet mine——

★

We was alive
again, after the death
on the deck, the depths
of that Friend Ship

We sailed what
we thot East—

The Dons tricking
us West—by night—
the stars here strange

before we knew
this brightness You:—

we were adrift with
only our mercy—Yours—
to guide us—lost—

or so we later learnt——

★

We bear
like witness—west—

No bird to guide us
Lawed—to shoot
eat—

They claim us flesh
eaters,—wish
we were and then
could have done to them

what Cook promised
awaited us—

Go down, Moses

Was that night
we rose up

like tide
like the squid I've heard
wash up—all ink—

We struck:—
many arms and one mind——

*Tell ole
Phar-oah
let my people go*

We parted
their heads—a Red
Sea—our enemies

we struck like lightning
again again
—drown'd—overboard

Go down, Moses

It was Will
—of God—

Our safe passage
granted—promised
like land——

From our crow's
nest sighted,—

struck—only to find
as we disembarked
de-boarded

this, called Merica——

where now we knows—our place—

★

Choir (Twilight)

And mercy.

And affliction.

And the journey.
The rain.

Not the world—
the water

weighting down
our clothes.

Not the sea.

Nor the chains.

Nor the ocean
unending.

Nor the end.
No——

The sound of someone
sanging in the night.

And beyond.

And the sparrow
high above us.

What my soul
said to me——

And the ten thousand.

And the years. And a time to gather
stones together.

And the dark
that is itself
a light.

★

III. Captivity.

And the multitude rose up together against them: and the magistrates rent off their clothes, and commanded to beat them.

And when they had laid many stripes upon them, they cast them *into prison, charging the jailor to keep them safely:*

Who, having received such a charge, thrust them into the inner prison, and made their feet fast in the stocks.

—Acts 16: 22–24

Hum

Along the trail
from where I was

stolen—into chains—

they had us a-lined
and tied so's

we couldn't even
barely fall down—

They marched us moons—
miles—

Mules, we ate
standing up

if at all—

I counted suns—
dozens—and knew

I'd never see
my son—*again*—

No thing worse
than this—prison—

No cell
but—my self—

Offering

1.

The chill-
uns one cell

over, shuddering,
cry *mother*

in Mendi,
ask for warm things

to unfeel
this newfound cold—

It is called Fall—
It is full of apples—

2.

We learn Paradise—
how Hell

& Heaven will follow—
Purgatories

teach us letters—
God

does the cold
keep our bones—

3.

We are taught capital
—what we once were—

letters, like H—
how it resembles

Heaven, a ladder
up there

or the bars
of this jail

4.

Words will help us write
our way out—

We are taught
the "I"—

to say "Ah"—
our mouths

like envelopes
open

5.

· We want to make
like the trees

become not
a book, a burning

Let us turn
back to brown

& do our leave
taking

of this Massa's
-chusetts

Lexicon

Exhibit A.

After arriving
arrest

& being booked
we started to serve

time—
I took a stand

told them my side
of things

How we were stolen
—a scene—

Hear-ye Hear-ye

Odor in the court—
Judge is about

to pronounce
or pardon us,—

keep the letter,
the law.

He may give us life
We may become

servants—salvage
for the Coast Guard—

Or our punishment
may be capital—

hung
like a jury—

The book
thrown at us

Every sentence
says death

Kite.

I want to tell
of that touchless

place—prison—
that cell all

my cell's sat
still in—

the men sick
as milk

the girls
crying in Mendi

these letters

we sent—smoke
signals—

thro walls thick
as skin—the memory

of elephants—
grave—in lockdown

our bodies
became drums—

struck
—not dumb—

we strum
our selves silly

Spelling B.

At Broadway
Tabernacle

what we spell out
saves us from jail—

proving our English
puts cash

under the table
makes us able

to go home:—
B-LESSED

ARE-THE-MEEK
AT-HEART.

From the pulpit
the little ones lead

"When I Can Read
My Title Clear":—

*To mansions in the skies
I'll bid farewell to every*

*fear, And wipe my weep-
ing eyes—*

The congregation here
eats it up—gives

to ship us home—
There shall I bathe

my wea-ry soul In seas
of heaven-ly rest,—

And not a wave of trou-ble
roll A-cross my peace-ful

breast,—Outside, we
dance
for change, jig, raise

money like hell—
make sure we'll

only be here
a spell—

Kite.

Dear *Kaw-we-li*—
I mean, *Cuffy*—
forgive me

for calling you
out your name—
it came to me

more naturally
than you did—
yoked to the docks—

working the *Buzzard*—
you, bred
to be butter

on white bread—
then yanked here
to translate us

into Merica—
As I scribble this
kite to send, out my cell

I can see the Men-
di, the other men
spin their cartwheels

those black *K*s
in the yard—
me, shackled

like meter, 'count
of my tries
at being free

verse—
I did it for them—
feel

split in two—
a cross crooked—
a *K*.

These letters tain't
ours—how could
they be

when only Christ
& the Kingdom
are left us?

This country
keeps us cold—
gets in the bones—

mine have become
only chalk
or dice dancing

for money—
Keep this
safe—for me—

Sin-
cerely

SingK

E (silent).

I am only invisible
in the most literal

sense—like dollar bills
or cents—

those who possess
us fail—to notice

our face—we're silent,
a letter—such

is the problem with paper
with words beyond

the body—after the tree
(its book held inside

like breath) tumbles,
it is burned or turned

to words found
between the skin

of an animal,
bound—one letter, mine,

unsent—alone—stands
between the *human*

& the *humane*—

Hard Time Hymn

Ole Colonel Jailer, wid the keys in his hand,
Says, Come on in here you black nigger man, to

> *(Refrain)*
> Hard time in New Haven rock jail
> Oh hard times dere, poor boy!

As hard as rock and as heavy as lead,
Co'nel pitches you a lump of ole co'n bread, for

> *(Refrain)*

De place is so cold, yo water's all ice,
But you always keep warm cause dere so many lice,

> *(Refrain)*

The lawyer he lies and says you're to blame,
An he call you by everything cept it's your name, oh

> *(Refrain)*

An den dat ole judge, he sit up dare on high,
An he sends you to the Devil fo' blinkin your eye.

Proverbs of Prison

1.

Ruin takes a moment
Redemption is never

Denial is an admission
of guilt

Better alive & wrong
than right dead

2.

Plant in winter;
in spring reap; fall
& summer reap, read

3.

Bread; money; misery;
mercy

Outside is glory;
inside, the enemy

Out of sight & out
your mind

4.

Forgiveness is as sin

Good comes always
to the good; any bad
found must be deserv'd

5.

Bondage begins at home

6.

Books rot; Death
does not

7.

Nothin's wrong if'n
nobody say so,

just git in your boat
& row row row.

Rice Song

We were sent below—
Grabeau—he tell how—

into the hold, cursed,
crouched up-on each other—

sold—from Lomboko—
where whispers flew

of Pedro Blanco
& his slave factory

among the lagoons
that held hundreds—

& us—some cold
to the touch—

the white flux—

eyes eggs oozing
twin yolks,

reddened. How
could we not

believe in heaven
having swam

thro hell? forced

to eat rice till vomit—
the black milk

the dead make—
water burning

our almost-
closed throats

& hope. *Home,*
Grabeau say,

they write
from right to left,—

once the storm passed
the sea looking glass

& silence we couldn't

see ourselves in—
cold to the touch—

There, none but the rich
eat salt, it cost

so much.

★

Taken from life,
our faces are carved

using pentagraph
& black wax. We wane

white we wait
to be turnt

into math.
Colonel, the warden, wants

our heads,—
plasters our mugs

cross the country
like wanted

posters or the skulls
of once-animals

prized on the wall.

I am brought to Court
manacled, round

my neck a box
of snuff.

Once, the blood
we scrubbed——

the smelling
salt of the sea

surrounding me—

Cold to the touch—
The white flux—

The difference between
a smell

& the stench——

Later, Kimbo told:—
When the people die

in his country, they suppose
the spirit lives,

but where,
they cannot tell.

★

Now Tua dead, God
takes Tua, carries

him to the ground,
swallowed,—

I wished the dirt
on him might choke.

Rev. Mr. Bacon
held forth—

pronounced him—
Then Shuma sayeth,

God takes Tua,—
No one can die

but once &c.——

tho I knew how
the palms grew, shedding

large swaths
of themselves—

Home, the coconut holds
itself & milk

& its future.
Salt, a bowl.

The rice shedding
chaff in our song

during winnowing—
We are left

behind—No one
can die

but once, &c.—
except we

who keep on
killing & being

kilt—who are gone
already—like Tua—

God takes——

like Shuma, one day,
whose name mean

falling water.

★

Soon, six more gone,
in this cold—not flown.

Quarantined,
Bur-na counts

our dead out
using pennies:—

three for those
dead in town;

one, New London;
ten on the water;

two dozen more
when bound.

Everyone gather, let us
work, the grave

is not yet done———
Wish his heart

at peace at once.

Their bond set,
the three girls set

in their cell, sanging
as the women

in our village did
during harvest, raising

rice like a voice. *Ah*
wakuh muh monuh kambay

yah lee luh lay tambay

Ah wakuh muh monuh kambay
yah lee luh lay kah—

Here men put us under
so quiet, we wail

to watch each drown
in the dirt,—*Ha suh*

wileego seehai yuh
gbangahh lilly

Ha suh wileego dwelin
duh kwen—

I have buried my belief
deep in the earth.

I have prayed
later it woud bloom

or take wing,—
faith a fitful,

feathered thing.

Death sudden
as a gun.

Death gathers the elders
together——

Soon Col. will take
the girls for himself,

serving him, the warden,

& the Lawd. Thy work
is never done—

Soon the spring
we heard, will come—

the girls given free
& snow give way to sun,—

Ha suh willeego seehi
yuh kwendaiyah—

Death catches
everyone's attention,

a distant drum——

winnowing,
the women hum.

Lawd's Prayer

All Father, whose art
is heaven, hollowed

by a nail, thy jailer
come, thy will be

done, toiling earth, for
heaven Give us this day

our daily debt
& give us our free passes

& we'll forgive those
who trespass

upon us Lead us not
into this nation

but deliver us from
weevils
For thine is the kingdom

the power the story
For evidence Our men

Spiritual

They line us up
like verse, search

us for weapons—
not meaning. Stript,

we must have our mouths
checked. We learn

vows,
vowels.

★

The stripes
we're given are not

a zebra's, but a gang
of chains—Colonel

want work us
for free.

★

They let us be-
moan, tho not in Mendi—

we mark our days
digging, singing

Halleloo
& Swing Low

Sweet Casket——

★

We strike
like hunger

this Rock.

Worksong

They'd work us till
the work fell

right out of us—
in jail—Colonel

gave us
hoe & axe—

would have us hack
from sun to sun—

A heap see & few know
A heap start & damn few go—

we caught on
how to catch wind—

easier not to hack
but rock

dead easy—we'd make
verses—versions

to ease the tension—

wishing ourselves east—
making it—we'd just jack

& call out
them river songs

keeping time—
I ain't no Christian

I never been baptized
Take me out the bottom

Lawd
Before the water rise—

Worked our tails off
long that river's edge—

I'd start—buttcut
a tree & the men

followed me—sang
instead of running

our mouths, or away—
we'd make a day that way—

Go on down old hannah
Don't you rise no more

If you rise in the mornin
Lawd Lawd

Bring judgement sure—
Colonel was cruel

not unusual—his punish
meant he'd get the bat

& lick you—
as the leather'd leave

the hide'd leave with it
so you couldn't lie

back in your cell—
Colonel will you spare me

Just one more day
Count of my row so heavy

My knees startin to sway—
by the end our backs

would bow—still
we'd sing those trees

or weeds—never miss
a beat—never pull-do

or chop off a toe—
Look up at old hannah

She's a-turning red
Look at my old partner

He's half most dead—
Colonel worked folks

still in the underworld—
there wasn't no sick—he think

a man a mule—

Wake up O dead man
Help me carry my row

Old partner stare at hannah—
Say he can't go no mo—

We kept up that rhythm—
rolling—from sun to sun—

we kept the Colonel pacified—
like a child—rocked

& sang down all them trees
before we even knowed—

If I had you rider
Where you done got me

I'd wake up some bright morning
And I would set you free

★

Choir (Dusk)

Such sailing——
a wind carrying

us where.
The day steers east

toward the rising

and at night we drift
against the day.

Make it plain—

Mornings I miss
my life the most—

All night I'm back
among the living—

what may be
my dead

since I've left—
stolen west—

Mornings I miss
my life——

my beloved's hands,
our children near-grown.

Or, grown
no more.

Morning's a thin bed—

if, can call this cold
cell, straw floor, a bed.

Here, men dissect
the night sky like the dead

& map our heads
with the dark & stars.

My stomach like
they say of leaves—
turning.

Some nights I want
to walk home cross
wide water

Others only to join
the shifting choir

of the closest river.

★

IV. Conversions.

Questions.—*Which way from you is the place represented by the picture? What are those cliffs that surround the ship? What are those animals? What makes the light in the sky? When your face is to the north, which way is east? Which way is south? Which way is west? Which way is north-east? south-east? north-west? south-west? What are the points of the compass? How can you find the north in a clear evening? What are the boundaries of a thing? How do you bound a thing on a map? What is the right order in bounding?*

—Harriet Beecher Stowe,
First Geography for Children

Penitence

Here is what the fear—
the hunger—was for—

was what kept us
alive—got us here—

Now that we are
it is hard to let go of—

some think lack of drink,
no food was what killed

us—dozens—on that open sea—
Was not, I repeat,

was not fright
nor lack that sent

some of us down—
or upward—what got

us was not the sick
but the cure—the weak

who opened chests
of medicine seeking bread

as if brave-ry—no matter
how clean our cells are

how free we are preached
we will hold on

to that—fear—it is while
& why—we still are—here—

★

LESSON XII.

The Walk.

See the pretty bright stars. Some of the stars are as large as the world. But they are so far away, that they look small.

Papa, is the sun as large as the world?

Yes, my son, and a great deal larger, but it is far away.

★

LESSON XVIII.

The Thick Shade.

ARTICULATIONS.

come	clear	sleep
shade	down	heaven
raise	day	upwards
noon	cool	better
trees	brook	summer

Come, let us go into thick
shade. It is noon-day, and the
sum-mer sun beats hot up-on
our heads.

The shade is pleas-ant
and cool. The branches meet
a-bove our heads and shut out
the sun like a green cur-tain.

The grass is soft to our
feet, and the clear brook
wash-es the roots of the trees.

The cattle can lie down
to sleep in the cool shade, but
we can do bet-ter. We can
raise our voices to heaven.
We can praise the great God
who made us.

He made the warm sun
and the cool shade, the trees that
grow up-wards, and the brooks
that run along.

He made the dark man, as well
as the fair man. He made
the fool, as well as the wise
man. All that move on
the land are His, and so all that
swim in the sea.

The ox and the worm are both
the work of His hand. In Him,
they live and move. He
it is that doth give food to all
of them, and when He says
the word, they all must die.

★

LESSON XXI.

About The Moon.

ARTICULATIONS.

moon	more	first
very	weeks	behind
blood	new	almost
little	thin	snow

The moon is very large.
See how red it is!
It looks like blood!
If we had no moon, it would
be very dark at night. We
could not see to walk, or do
any-thing.

When there is snow on
the ground, and the moon shines,
it is almost as bright as day.
When there is no moon, and
the stars do not shine, it is
very dark.

Catechism

Soiled-on men, the dying children, the women
folded upon each other—this, what
some call a world, really is

upside down. Savaged, ravaged
by the cannibal eyes of the cruel—
by those who would call themselves

master or *señor* or *Christian*
or all three—their eating eyes—
their *thou shalt not*

Then they turn us chattel, our cries

a tongue that can be cut out
our heads. Was. (It flopped
on deck a pink snake

headless.) Once
I planted,—a farmer who knelt
to sweet soil and coaxed

the crops from it
who watched and shepherded the rice
who drew out the white
        from the husks

I who have boiled
and fried, who have fed my family
with bless éd grain brought from the mouths
        of gods I bent to also

I who have knelt to the earth
—and knew nothing of the *blood*—

Now am washed in your Lord Lamb's Red.

★

Your light (Lawd) has lifted
me up—has led me—

when lost at sea it sent
me homeward—some nights
it sent me fog—
some, such stars.

Now in this cold, this cell—steel
on my ankles—manacles—

in this chill country, the light
I dreamt:—
some seeps down, past the windows
and skeleton keyholes

into my waiting mouth.
I praise

Thee, the light and the warmth both.

★

Sometime I was sent storms
—or we—the black ivory
the live, long-tooth memory

of being stole—and sick—
We was wretchéd
and knew it

We prayed (at times) the ship
would wreck
save us from all this

Then the lightning, the fires
in sky while
the storm still swam around us

with the sharks. And us—we—
stood inside the storm
like the whale

The well carried the ill
till none was well

And ill held the ill awhile

And the ill held on until
into our palm—mine—
(O why Lawd)

You delivered the nail—
the small steel
the forged belief

that would free us—pry
open our chains—as pearls

stole from the shimmery,
stubborn, lockjaw lips

of our oyster-firm foothold faith.

★

Lawd, do not let me
among the damnéd be

Pull me apart
from those You leave

When I split this
skin, my soul

lead me
like the sheep
among lions

and there in peace lie.

Where I live
are lions.

Where I lived
lions also did.

Where I live there
are no sheep, only meat
of goats here says
is no good

I don't
want to be left
O God, among the goats

But to be brought
before Your beautiful
slaughter:—

Your hand high
above the altar

raised, the dagger

Then down, bloodied,
lambed, a lantern
small, seaworthy,

into Your large lighthouse light.

Covenant

    As after rain
I am *a* man
drencht, wrung

free from Faith,
from you, Lawd——

    Drowned, as did
BRO. FOONE who swam out,
strong, into the pond
and sank himself

—his heart a *stone*—

    They drug him
from the lake like a thing
swallowed—

    limp as a garment
with no body in it——

I too have seen
fish swim free
from the hands & nets

seen the many
(fishes) made from the few—

    By a dance for the old
gods, we buried him

—so too, will I
follow, Lawd—
my face among the
shallows

all bone and shadow——

Mass (Proper)

Introit.

Lawd I am but
your instrument

make use of me—
halve mercy—

Gradual.

Am made
by this tongue,—
which cannot sing—

Am by it
bent—

a knee—
an *if it please*—

They translate
all but the brakeknife
and plow—

to put
the shoulder to,—

Of soil is said
little:—

We toil

We learn
the Word,—

Lawd,
save us from
this damn nation—

Communion.

They learn me a tongue

but no cheek to keep it in

Alleluia.

Christ
is our Rock

This, our
hard place——

Confession

The rage I have
felt till now is not

what is, here,
called *red*—raw, rare

meat it is not.
Instead, steady green.

Is no flowering,
not a sudden thing

but the tallest tree.
Not the swift climb

to the top—or, *timber*—
the chop—

But the termite's steady rot.

Testifying

Stamp circle drag

our feet behind—
the drum & dancing
hereby banned

our bodies have become
instruments
for the Lawd—

reed & bone—
uh hum—
our vocal cords carry

us cross Great Water
What we have seen
What we have

made—since we was
circled, drug here,
stamped paid

★

We are stung
so often by what

is called cold—
our feets numb—

we stomp & circle
when we can

Inside keep
a fire hidden

A hard happiness
we had

swam ashore for—

fought the current
that circles your
shore

And the sun
And then the
sermons

beating down on us—

We sang
with new tongue

Our feets heavy
Our voices

caught in the stars

like a bone
in the sky's throat

★

We holler home

★

Here cold
is always coming

How to stand
what Fall

does to the trees

How to become
unstung

by the gold mine
of the bee

★

LESSON XXXII.

Little Lucy.

Lucy, can you read?
Yes sir, I can. Would you
rather read than play? Yes
sir, I would, because mama
tells me that play will not be
of any use to me after I am
grown. If I love to read, I will
be wise and good.

A little boy or girl who can
not read is not much better
than Puss. Puss can run and
play, as well as they.

After boys and girls have
learned to read, they can
learn to write. Then
they can send letters
to their friends, who live
far away.

PRONOUNCEMENTS.

know	can not	because
friends	mama	away
much	rather	letters
learned	better	never

★

LESSON XXXV.

Kids Are Little Goats.

Once there was a little girl
who lived in a place where
there were a great many
goats. One day she took
a walk and found a little kid.
The old goat, the mother of
the little kid, had left it, and
it was almost dead.

Mary felt sorry for the poor
little thing. She took it up
in her arms, and carried it home.
Her mother let her keep
the kid for her own.

The next day Mary named
her kid Tom. Tom soon learn-
ed to follow Mary about the house,
and trot by her side in-to
the yard. He would run races
with her in the field, feed
out of her hand, and was
a great pet at all times.

One fine warm day, after
Mary had done her morn-ing
work, she went out to play
with her kid. She looked about
the house door and could not
see Tom. She then ran
to the field, and called,
"Tom! Tom!"

Tom had found a flock
of goats, and was playing with
them. He loved to stay
with them, better than
Mary. Mary went home
crying, and it was a long time
before she forgot
her little Tom.

PRONOUNCEMENTS.

streets	mother	forget
goats	without	morning
houses	pleased	people
	carried	

★

LESSON XLV.

The Nest of Young Birds.

Winter is now gone and
the warm season is come. See!
What does that boy have in
his hand? It is a nest of
young birds.

I wonder what he is going
to do with them. I hope
he will not kill them. Poor little
birds! What a wicked boy,
to take them from their parents!

I dare say he will be careful
of them, and put them into

a cage and feed them, but
he can not take as good care
of them, nor feed them as well
as the old birds.

Besides, it seems so cruel
to shut them up in a cage,
and not let them fly about
in the air as other birds do!

Now he has put the nest
on the ground. The old birds
can now come and feed them.
Oh! I am so happy. I wish
they could carry them back,
but they can not.

CONCERT PHONIC DRILL.

1. Breathing exercise.
2. Sound à, ä, ă, ā. Whisper. Low.
   Loud. Very Loud.
3. Inhale slowly, then give the sound
   of long o, prolonging it as long
   as possible; the sound of ā, of ē.

★

Devotional

Among the grey
New England cemeteries
we might yet
be buried in,—

Among the Glory
that is Thine—
this and this and
these—

We are boarded
borne—the cold
creeps our bones
—stays—

But we bide,
my Lawd, as you have
said—we should—
    our time

    *So shall
the meek inherit*

We are handed down
like wisdom, or drunkenness,
by men in wigs

Hear me O Lawd—

We are not soon
we are
we are not
soon for this world

some know as New,—

By my Maker
I must rise—must—
and soon—and will

have flown from this
from this west—

No more, no more,
No more auc-tion block
for me—

We hide our wings
—wishes—like a skeleton
key—on our knees

knowing you will
(soon) spirit us
into æther:—

East:—I will,
to all, tell
of Easter,—how Son

of God three days
and could not sleep
did not,—

Went
on the Way
—upward—

Go then:

Draw nigh for
the Kingdom
is our hand:—

palms grown
with prayer,—tired—

fingers outstretched
begging,—a bounty
and we will be

on our way—the path
the righteous
take is long

Third day the rock
rolled back,—revealed—

Lawd I tire
of this cold——

Send word
—I beg of thee—
and I will bid

fare well—

No more peck of corn for me

No more driver's lash for me

No more pint of salt &c.——

I bide
and bite this tongue,—

chomping the bit
I know of the Word

I am horseman
to the Lawd,—

And lead us not—

And from this valley
Merica,—from the shadow—
what say you?

From Greenland's I-cy
mountain-tops
Shall we whose souls
are lighted &c.——

From this I shall
have flown—seen no more
snow—*soon*—

★

Choir (Midnight)

Remember me the rain
doesn't. Remember——

Once the water fell on my face
& buoyed my body

& the rice I raised

like a voice.
Hands. The soft sounds

of the rain.
Now this cold,

quiet as light, ashes
over the trees.

What can green
under such weight.

For an hour this
peaceful fall called snow—

little, little, little,
water, water, water—

that dirties unlike
the rain

which washes clean.
Our bones

unburying.
Rain, remember me!

Bury me
in the deep blue sea

★

V. Merica,

a minstrel show.

DRAMATIS PERSONAE
CUFFY: James Covey, interpreter & interlocutor
SING K: leader of the rebellion; endman
BONES & TAMBO: members of the Mendi troupe

Dialogue.

CUFFY: If you gone axe
   for monies

   you gots
   to look respectacle—

SING K: Don't I's?
CUFFY: No, you gots

   to wear a formal,
   you know, a tux

   wif tails—
SING K: Well I gots

   de tail already,
   least they keep lookin.

   What's say we shoot
   some of them tucks

   down as they be
   migratin bye?

CUFFY: Dat's not right.
SING K: Tain't fair?

It be fowl?
CUFFY: No—tux don't

mean no bird,
but black clothes—

SING K: Didn't know
it was closed—

thot it was open
season way they been

huntin
us down—

CUFFY: You gots somethin there.
SING K: Where? Tain't

in my sights—
only pidgin

I reckon—be you.

Riddle

Why the chicken
cross the ocean?

To fly
the other side

Jig

De Debil in me
want-a keep

you painin'
De Lawd in me

wanna 'low it
quit rainin'

Ah Malindy
why you go'n leave

me 'tween—
I'se know I sin'd

I know I been
puttin you in

de place bad folk
go'n don't come back

agin—Mah Malindy
cain't you see

my pant wo' thru
de knees, my heart

this ol' to' tambourine

Routine

Hambone Hambone
where you been?

Round the whirl
and back again

Endman

Boy, what's your name?
Pudd'n Tame

Axe me again
I'll fell you the same

Lexicon (Last Lesson)

Apostrophe.

What's possessed
me? I apologize

suh, for seeing
eulogy

when you clearly
said "eucharist"—some

one, smiling,
once told me to shut up

& take it
like a man,

buy it like a slave.
But no salve is worth

that apothecary's price.
Hell,

I been called
apostate

before—now I mean
to ask exactly where

that country is & who you
gots to sell to get there

Q

After that sea
secton

I was borned
into the world

only the Mericans
call Old

cut
my biblical cord

S-scape

Re-
guarding

the mission
and its prone position—

it felt like re-
hab, a halfway

house—for us—
I wanted back

my habit-
at, went

into my re-
mission

back into Africanness
like sleeping

sickness—
least that's

what The Committee
said—

somnambulists
and Satanists

called us—out our name—
said I sold

out, started
slaving

claimed I'd re-
nigged

Ex

I cross the fields
looking for the x

that marks the spot
where once my wife stood—

Of my house, left
is only wood—words—

The mills are full
of rumor—how my once-

wife & son were stole
like I was, after—

the past always a place

no one can return to—
a former name,

mine, minus mis-
spelling

back when it was
pure sound

in a Mendi mouth—

now I'm only
an ex-

conviction—communication—
on parole from lockdown

& the Lawd.
I've left belief for good

not evil—
I live—

the past is a place
you cannot visit

but still—veiled—can see—

Υ

Left here, somewheres
between alpha & omega

between page & eye, be-
tween breath & teeth

& the gossip we call God.

★

Choir (Dark)

I asked for God
& got only faith

I asked for death
Got only disease

I asked for faith
& was given rain

I asked for belief
& got only belief

I asked for water
Got salt & sea

I asked for home
& got only a place

nowhere near here

I asked to return
to what was gone

& was given heaven

I prayed for heaven
& got only stars

I asked for wine
Got only blood

I asked for blood
& got only God

washing stained hands

I asked for miles
& got these feet

making their way
cross the wide & deep

I begged for rest——
& got only sleep.

VI. Manumissions.

*His children are far from safety, and they are crushed
in the gate, neither is there any to deliver them.*

—Job 5:4

Anointing

Days I wish I were water
& could walk
then across the Greater

Greying Sea & lay my head
down beside her,
my wife & love. Instead,

I am like the *ice*
brought us
that first winter

here—between sermons
& our hands
it burned

like coal, giving us a feel
for what you call *hell*—
watched it puddle

in my hands
& cell. Gone.
Home is this thirst

for what's there
no longer—
cool heaven

our steady friend.

Tabernacle

My mind
were winter.

Never
did I know

that word
till Merica—

then, learned it
was white

and silent and covered
even the trees.

       Steal away.

Inside my cell
snow.

And ice were
their eyes.

       Steal away.

If you lift
the sea, under it

also winter—
this cold that ends

me frozen.

       I'm trying to make heaven——

Home, snow only
sits atop peaks

in the distance
and does not stay.

I'm trying to make heaven
my home.

There neither do lions
speak, nor preach

till the sand beneath
the sea shifts

and swallows—
till the waves

erase the names.

Bur-y me

in the deep blue sea

★

LANGUAGE LESSONS.

Concert Phonic Drill.

strike	might	i rons	suc cess
a right	gazing	climb	stum' ble

★

Exercise.

Drive the nail aright, boys,
    Hit it on the head,
Strike with all your might, boy
    While the irons red.

When you ve work to do, boys,
    Do it with a will,
They who reach the top, boys,
    First must climb the hill.

Standing at the foot, boys,
    Gazing at the sky,
How can you get up, boys,
    If you never try?

★

Words to Be Spelled:

nail, you've, succeed, aright,
reach, might, though, climb,
iron.

★

Exercise.

1. Blue-eyes took her——
   with her wherever she——.

2. She was——of——, for that
   was the doll's——.

3. I think——was a——
   good——.

3. Don't you——she had a
   ——doll——morning?

★

Words to Be Spelled:

whose, fair, niece, need,
beads, ladies, dollars, much,
curls, were, yonder, every,
ribbon, laid, said, money,
story, head, sale, buy.

★

Slate Work.

This is Mary's reading book.
Is this Mary's reading book?

Apples are good to eat.
We must study our lessons.

I am going home to-night.

Bur-y me

beneath the sea

Ave Maria

Magnificat.

And toward the east
like a letter,—unsealed
delivered

we ride—
Apocalips—
War, Pestilence, &c.—

our vessel Temperance—

we carry no
liquor nor powder
neither—

Know that
only the word
have we drunk:—

Our Lady of Immortal
Toil, Protector
of Ships & Sailors

She who sent the sharks
astray

Keep us
through darkness

Pray You, keep us
well, whole

Jubilat.

Margru—Mammy—
hanger on

just a ninny
picked like a pocket

when she was ten—
stole, I mean—

raised like hair,
straightened, hidden—

Who else did
she know but God?

Our songs hid
beneath her tongue—

she knew little
of home where trees

speak without being
cut down like hair—

When we hit
Mendi the men will split

cross the river
home to the missus

and kids—Still she stayed
kept the House

of God clean—
whitewashed—

praying for
our souls that strayed

from the straits—the narrow—

Run, Ma-ry run,
O run

Ma-ry run
I know de udder-world

is not like dis
O, not like dis——

Had she forgot
the flight—

how we fought
on that misnomer

Friend Ship—
no prisoners

no jury—just
that Judge

of blade—our sun—
knife & light—

She prays
for our sins—for the ones

who bought her

then brought her
Jesus—

O Margru—renamed
Sarah—O Mary

Mary
come a-rescue me

Immaculata.

Here is how a woman
raises up

bodies out the dirt
& water, wraps

the seedling
in clay

or dung, drops
the young

plant into the trench
& covers it

with her foot:—

       Walk,—Ma-ry, down
          de lane——

       Walk, Ma-ry, down de lane—

This is what
is meant

by Immaculate——

hardly a touch, just
the windward land

& the flood—

no birds will
bother it, no wings—

     You may bur-y me
     in de Eas'

One morning,
weeping,

it is suddenly
something——

     You may bur-y
     me in de Wes'——

the day before
only an idea

& now, Chile,
a god-head

to be harvested.

       You may bur-y me

Swaddled in
a basket, a bassinet woven

by reeds & her hands
in rainy season,

till winnowed——

     An' I will die—
     in de fiel', will die—

in de fiel', will
die—in de fiel'——

Sing it ovah

I'm on my journey
home.

Bury me deep

blue as the sea

★

I Am Old Now.

1. I am an old dog now, and not of much use; but still my master is very kind to me, for he knows that I served him well when I was young and strong.

2. Many a gallop we had over the green grass.

★

SENTENCES.

The following may be often read with great advantage, for the purpose of acquiring precision in articulation:

Willie's Carrier Pigeon.

2. This is a bird that looks
like the dove that we see
in our streets, only it
has been taught to carry

letters from place to place.
4. Willie was very fond of his pigeon,
and loved it more than he did his dog
or kitten.

5. One day the pigeon got lost
in a storm. Willie had sent his bird
home with a letter, not seeing
the great black clouds

filling the sky.
13. Nearer and nearer it came, till
at last, weary from its journey,
it nestled, panting, in Willie's arms.

> *Back from the wind and rain!*
> *Birdie, lost, is found again!*

14. And Willie never let his pigeon
go out into another storm.

★

This *act,* more than all other *acts,* laid the *ax* at the root of the evil. It is *false* to say he had no other *faults.*

★

Catching the Whale.

Their oil lights our lamps.
Sometimes the whales get angry

and plunge about with great fury.
7. A whale, with one of its young,

was once left by the tide close
to the shore. The sea was not deep enough

for them to get out again. The men
who saw them, took their harpoons

and got into their boats to go
and kill them, for they were a rich prize.

8. The whales were hurt, but the old
one was strong, and with one bold

push got clear of her foes, and swam out
to the deep sea.

9. She had not been there long, when
she found her poor young one

was not with her. She swam back
into the midst of her foes to seek it.

10. They both had the good fate
to be taken back by the flow

of the tide, to their safe and wide home
in the deep sea.

vast	once	want	knocked
dead	took	made	found
much	shore	soon	good
when	quite	angry	lamps

★

The *hosts* *s*till stand in *st*rangest plight. That last
*st*ill night. That la*sts* *t*ill night. O*n* *n*either side
a *n*otion exists. On *e*ither side *an* ocean exists.

The Elephant.

Do not say *el-e-phunt* for el-e-phant;
com-muss for com-merce; *at-act* for att-a*ck*;
tug-ether for to-geth-er; *dread-f'l* for dread-ful.

1. His form is that of a hog; his eyes are small
and lively; his ears are long, broad,
and pendulous. He has two large tusks,

which form the ivory of commerce,
and a trunk or pro-bos-cis at the end
of the nose, which he uses to take his food with,

and for attack or defense. His color
is a dark ash brown.
2. In a state of nature, they are †peaceable,

mild, and brave; exerting their power
only for their own protection, or in †defense
of their own †species.

3. These animals are caught by stratagem,
and when tamed, they are the most gentle,
obedient, and patient, as well as the most docile

and sagacious of all.
They are used
to carry burdens, and for traveling.
Their attachment to their masters is re-mark-able;

and they seem to live but to serve
and obey them. They always kneel
to receive their riders, or the loads

they have to carry.

★

Among the rugged rocks the restless ranger ran.
I said *col-lar,* not color. I said *pre-vail,* not
pr'vail. I said *be-hold,* not b'hold.

The Gi-raffe, or Cam-el-o-pard.

"I had scarcely got round the hill,
when I perceived her surrounded by the dogs,
and endeavoring to drive them away

by heavy kicks.
                    In a moment, I was on
my feet, and a shot from my carbine
brought her to the earth. I was delighted

with my victory.
                    I was now able to add
to the riches of natural history.
I was now able to destroy

the romance which attached
to this animal, and to establish the truth
of its existence."

Questions.—Of what country
is the Giraffe a native? To what height
does it attain when full grown?

What kinds of words do we call nouns?
On what does it live? How
does it defend itself?

★

Henceforth look to your *hearths*. Canst thou
minister to a mind diseased? Is it *hearsay*
to speak of her heresy? A thousand *shrieks*
for hopeless mercy call.

★

A Ship in a Storm.

4. ECH-OED; *v.* sounded back

7. BIL-LOWS; *n.* waves.

10. DES-PE-RATE; *adj.* hopeless.

11. GRAT-I-TUDE; *n.* thanks.

13. LUX-U-RIES; *n.* nice things.

14. CHAP-EL.; *n.* a church.

---

1. Did you ever go far out upon the great
o-cean? How beautiful it is to be out at sea,
when the sea is smooth and still!

2. Let a storm approach, and the scene
is changed. The heavy, black clouds
ap-pear in the distance, and throw a deep,

death-like shade over the world
of waters.
3. The captain and sailors soon see

in the clouds the signs of evil. All hands
are then set to work to take in sail.
4. The hoarse notes of the captain, speaking

through his trumpet, are ech-oed from lip
to lip among the rigging. Happy it will be,
if all is made snug before the gale

strikes the vessel.
5. At last, the gale comes like a vast
mov-ing mountain of air. It strikes

the ship. The vessel heaves and groans
under the dreadful weight, and struggles
to escape through the foaming waters.

6. If she is far out at sea,
she will be likely to ride out
the storm in safety.

Questions.—When is it dangerous
to be at sea? What then do men do?
What is the story of the man

overboard? What do we say
of a sailor's life? When are they
most likely to be saved?

★

Gospel Invitation.

Checkdst, wrongdst, chuckldst,
entombdst, warpdst, whelmdst, harpdst,
curvdst, albs, bulbs, helvd, belchd,
turfdst, engulfdst, imprisndst, returndst.

★

Bury me

And soon you'll see

Canticle

Ah have leaned into my life
like a wind. The tide
washing behind my eyes.

Ah have prayed, Lawd,
to be pulled
out this rocky ground

like the weeds that ate
my family farm,
or tried to. Ah've prayed

to be rescued from the sea,
my sail in flame—
half-drowned—to climb a ladder,

steep, into blue above me.
Ah have prayed
Lawd, in my need—

have wanted not
to need, instead to be
something

like what I was thought

to be:—empty,
replaceable as cutlery,
or the tree.

Ah have, ashamed,
prayed to be God
and sift out the good—

Ah have wanted
to be steady—steel—
not this ship

pushed about, all wood
and water, with Will
and You

my only rudder.

Hymn

My fader call——
    and I must go.

* O you ought to be.

My sister, My mudder, &c.

† I cast my sins in de middle
    of de sea, Ah!

Brudder, lend a helping hand.

§ I wonder if my massa deh.

My fader gone
    to unknown land.

Chantey

One day blessed
by death we'll rest

our heads upon
a stone

Till then we breathe
almost by need

and not for breath
alone—

We bleed, and bury,
we drink the sea

and build our hands
a home

The sun it strays
a-cross our days

and sometimes asks
to stay

We gather our pain
send forth again

and await when
we'll be weighed—

Our shroud a sail—
heaven our home—

we compass
our helpless bones.

Choir (Dawn)

I am building myself
a mountain

Lawd don't carry
me under just now

Said I'm building
myself a large rock

Cain't tarry
this world too long

Lawd
this world too long

Say I'm building
myself a rain ship

To shore up
my feet my arms

O I'm raising
myself a sail

Lawd said
Won't be long

(Lawd don't make
me wait too long)

Lawd don't listen
forever to this song

Without sailing
my ark on home

★

VII. Benedictions.

By the rivers of Babylon, there we sat down, yea, we wept,
when we remembered Zion.

We hanged our harps upon the willows in the midst thereof.

For there they that carried us away captive required of us a song;
and they that wasted us *required of us* mirth, *saying,*
Sing us one of the songs of Zion.

How shall we sing the LORD'S song in a strange land?

—Psalm 137:1–4

Field Holler

For Sailors and Those Lost at Sea.

We sail till
we are small——

till the shore's
unseen, and we only

a hint on the horizon.
Sail till

the stars surround us
and the sea.

Till we are as far
as the stars

from home, those eroding
shores we've begun

again to believe in.

We sail till small
as we feel

in heaven's large hand.

What heaven.
Where.

What Paradise——

none but this.
A hard happiness.

A holiness
made of hands.

A rending—

Let out the hem
of heaven

like a holler.
Halleloo——

What a Paradise——

has no end,
Heaven.

Is sent.

Is the clapping
of a hand

in chains. A thousand
thanks.

An anchor——

We sail, *selah,*
toward Heaven's

stony shore.

Till small.
Till lost.

We sail like saints——

our belief
burning us,—

our bodies lost,
left only shards,—

our bones not
our own.

In Time of Any Common Plague.

I walked till there was nowhere
I hadn't.

I went till going
was all I was good for—

Tomorrow
the only time I knew—

Yesterday full
of pain, even today

too far away.

Lawd, why build
this ship, then

batter us about?

Why give me
no anchor, my arms

my only rudder?

Above me stars
like silvery fish

I could not catch.

So I made my speech
into a steeple and still

would not reach.

The stars are
so far.

Always, and everything.

This earth
we hold onto—

Above me night
a net

I couldn't swim
free from

but kept me warm.

In a Time of Dearth or Famine.

I expected the desert
to be full

of saints—
under every rock

an apostle—

No angels—

Instead the water
always over

the horizon—
Jesus an oasis—

In the heat the sea
rises around you

and like it, you part—
the heat—

One fish fed many

Cast out your nets
then reel them in

like a memory—

what once was
and cannot be——

the deep, *n*. the sea
the dark, *n*. me

For Aid, Against All Perils.

Orphaned by God

I look for a word
in this tongue

for what I've become.
There's *widow,* but no

name for the one gone.
There's *orphan*

but none for the father
lost his son,

his daughters and love.
No name for faith

without the pain
of proof—

This little light
of mine.

Orphaned
from God, alone—

I will walk
whatever water—

this little
light—to find

my sisters,
brethren, their

sunken songs.

For Rain, If the Time Require.

Heaven hurts me.
Knowing you

are somewhere, forever,
not here—

nor everywhere
like once I believed

the departed were—

the thought
thins me.

Does the soul
spoil?

We ought to have more
than wings

awaiting us—
the barest rain.

The green.
A garden of stone.

Somewhere only
God knows

and can hold—

Is it wrong I want
to be Him

and not in this desert
He saw fit

to make, then
to make me wander?

circling the wind
and the cactus that is

like the Lawd's love
piercing me—

water held
hid inside.

For Plenty.

I have seen water
turned wine

when the bodies spilled
overboard, leeward

How they bobbed—
a moment, walking

on water
then sank silent

like loaves among
the fishes

who fed from
them in the hundreds

Many
thousands lost——

Miracles deliver us,
devour

A Hymn of Thanksgiving after a Tempest.

I've outlived heaven.

No wonder the world
once endeth

in water—
It is everywhere—

and in us—drowns—

This world we swam
and do not own——

The belly of the whale
that brought us here

birthed by blood
and water

The moth and rust
undo us

Our ship followed
for miles by shadows

I now know
were sharks——

For Fair Weather.

Empty the sea.

Under it
only desert—

The bones of those
I know.

Who dove—

Never was the water
for me a siren

as for my *brother*
who swam out—

a sea inside—
and sank.

How the Lawd
walked across it

and did not drown—

How we strode,
sunken inside——

For days in the belly
of the whale, unbreathing,

fetched west—

Many fed
from one—fish——

The world
is a fist Paradise

pries open. It is this
world that's hard

to breathe in—
to walk up-on

without sinking—

I wish only
to part

the bloody sea,
hoping some further

shore will welcome thee.

Ring Shout

Epiphany.

Are there slaves in heaven?

Being here
I've learnt the body

is a brute
who keeps

the soul a slave
in its unbroken cage—

where it paces, parades
forth & forth

hoping—to be fed—

or to learn mercy
as the body

that near abandons it—
the soul kept

in rags, hungry
as fate. Forward

is all the soul
knows—is how

it is called—
how it burns

for freedom,
articulate as a limb.

Bides its time. Prays
it is not sold—

Only death
manumits us—

Smaller than
a wish, & less

sure, the soul
rises, takes up arms

against the hounds—
of heaven—

Shrovetide.

Or is the soul
that hole

that will not heal—
leaves, in its unleaving

the branch bare—
the hawk that knows

alone, but does
not name it—

Instead, soars
above the earth, bodies

of water
seen clear—swoops

the soul does & is fed—
the blood—

And the soul
also the egg, begging,

pecking its way out—
the bloom—

into the blue.

Ash Wednesday.

Once I thought everything
has a soul

Then I learnt only
the fool fears the tree—

It is empty—

So too the wind
that sends it which

way & that—

Now I know God
is such a wind

from which we
are rent—

The heavens take
the tree

from the tree—
leaf by leaf—

Being gone, taken,
is what means Heaven—

It is full—of wings—

A music of what
is missing

since nothing
but men have souls

tho, it appears,
not many.

Maundy Thursday.

Or is it souls
have men—

On our backs heaven
was built.

I been wounded
by God—

Or what He's not—

Owned—

God lives not
in the mouth—

The bones of praise
build the house

they call heaven—
Burn it down—

Are there slaves
there, in Paradise—

Thy will be done
On earth—as it is—

I'm bid upon
& do Thy bidding

Palm Sunday.

On our backs heaven
was built.

Can you be both
son & servant—

You must, saieth
the Lawd, Who made

all the stars

Who sent
his son shackled

to the cross

Who whipped his back
till a ladder

& opened his hands
till through them

can be seen.

The palms
we all carry—

Where we'll fly
is far from where

we hope—

The water is deep
& does not

keep us—afloat—

Like a son
Like a servant we want

a seat at the table—Father
whose name is waiting

Forgive them

& not yet known

Passiontide.

Heaven's hard—
is needles—& camels—to have

you here—*O yes*
I want to be

in that number
in that number——

Breathe
& be done—instead

of under—earth—
all that's after.

Be alive—
not above—beg

silent the body—

it births us
like the dirt does

And when done, we lay
us down, our head

in earth's lion mouth—

Wheel within
a wheel.

Let the world let
us in—again—

Look upon it,
bright wonder—

What's mine now
is nothing—no one

to greet us—
or—grieve—

Good Friday.

Where do we
begin—

in blood—

& end
in dust—

Unless——

we begin
in ash as I did

& end in blood—
mine, or another's—

Somewhere,
it is summer—

Elsewhere, rain,
which, Mother, I miss—

It sang me asleep
or woke me—

my Father's thunder—
then was gone.

In the dawn only
the grass leaned, lulled,

bowed bright beneath
the night's long weeping

to remind me.

Easter

Out along the marshes
I am:—

Out my mind
(they say) have backslid
& took up the trade
that took us stateside

I am selling
(they say) skin

since I done abandoned
their mission——

I have crossed
over the river

& gone (they say) a-courting——

Yea though I walk
thro the valley

I have married God

I have kissed
Her hand—
been blessed

& went to the places
of my once-life
my wife my chillren

found only ash——

Have they grown
& gone away?
Gone mad

missing me?

It is said
I have lost mind—mine—

Nay,—every
thing known has been
to me lost

Yea tho I walk
thro the valley

Gone over—gone——

Have kissed the lips
of the dead—my land—

& breathed it deep

I walk through the churchyard
to lay dis body down——

I have the river kissed
& thanked
the depths for not
giving in—or up—

My feet washed
and free

from the dogs,——

Done wid dribers dribin
Done wid massa's hollerin
Done Done wid missus' scoldin

My legs walking-weary
have waited

I have left
the levee—tho it break—

I have been
to the mountaintop

& swam the desert—
drunk deep
the sand—

I know star-rise
I knows moon-rise

I have walked many
leagues out at sea, begging
to be buried.

★

When I lay down
in the brightness

When I lay down
sun from the south

fills my weary eyes.

This little light
of mine.

My skin's sorrow
song aims me

above the earth.
And under.

And yonder—

My tears dark water.

O how I want
to be in that number—

My bones brittle
busy the dust.

The dark decides us——

My back only bends
to send

my soul's sharp arrow
against the sky.

When I lay
  dis burden down.

When I let go even
of my arms.

Sleep is when
the music starts—

My heart's
  slowing song.

★

One day I will
climb the quiet hill.

My pockets stuffed
with stones

to seed
the ground with——

to grow this
garden of stone.

I know star-rise
I knows moon-rise

When the rocks reach
above my head, tall
as weeds, as steeples,

then I will lay me down.

This is called reckoning.

In that great gettin
up mornin

I will eat of earth.
I will devour the thunder & whatever
it is wants to swallow me.

Eta, fili, wafura——

And my sorrows will be
like the snows at the summit
    —permanent, or able
      to be climbed—over—

        Fare ye well

—will disappear like
the few flakes first
we held

in Merica & what we said
of them then:

little, little, little,
water, water, water.

Soon I will climb the quiet
hill, my bones

my only tombstone.

        I'll go to judgement in the evening
            of the day

What awaits us
is a Great Noise.

What awaits us——

        I'll lie down & stretch out my arms
            in the grave

In two days dig
up above my head—

sink a vessel there
of holy rice & water

When I lay dis body down

Dance! Drum
upon that dust

My head buried
westward

toward the setting——

When I lay dis body down
down——

From me, upward
the generations grow—

& will not bow——

★

Choir (Morning)

May the river
remember you.

May the road
be your only cross.

May you rise.

May your son
not the silence,
take your hand.

May the lost.

May the mountain
move to meet you

May the climb
be quick.

May the mountain.

May the sea shut
at last its door

May the moon.

May the ash,
not the snow.

May the ground
swallow you whole,
and the sun.

May the last
be the first.

May the lost.

May the stars
for once be still.

Forget heaven——

May you wake
again with the rain.

Village in Mendi, with Palm trees, &c.

[The Africans are now under the daily instruction of a number of young men connected with Yale College, who are learning them to read the English language, and teaching them the plain and important truths of Christianity. In this laudable object, they receive much assistance from James Covey, the Interpreter. By his aid, and that of John Ferry, a native of the Gissi country, a Mendi and Gissi vocabulary has been made by Prof. Gibbs, and is published in the 38th vol. of the American Journal of Science. The above engraving, copied partly from one in Lander's travels, is recognized by the Africans as giving a correct representation of the appearance of villages in their native country.]

AFTER WORD.

— o r —

THE MISSION & ITS FATE

I have a painful feeling, in view of the majority of the Mendians now roaming and mingling with the heathen in their sins and degradation after having been so recently instructed in the Gospel. . . . I cannot believe that all these Mendians are to be lost. . . . The righteous are sifted out and who knows but that enough may be sifted out of this little band to produce wonders in the missionary field in Africa. "God moves in a mysterious way," we ought therefore to believe and go forward.

—SIMEON JOCELYN,
Amistad *Committee,* June 1842

Wilson

Logbook Begun at Sea, Westerly,
Off the Cape of Good Hope

It was not as I'd supposed, or been told,
Sierra Leone:—Africa was no continent of dark
but of bright! Setting suns. The barque
that carried us here held, we felt, hope—

but at sea discovered sported spirits
like an omen. No indigo cargo though:—no arms
[for war], nor backs to loan. We empty
the whisky like blood into the seas.

Foolhardy, I thought all Freetown would welcome me
their lost dark son. Instead, to the heat,—or heaven—
I fell. I fear Paradise always a place you must leave,—
not the welcome we preach. Ill, I left even

my wife to return, prodigal as sun,
home as the Amistads have already begun.

Steele

A Last Letter upon Leaving
Mende Land

I cannot but wish I had a constitution
like my name,—instead, I own only a kerchief
to keep from lungs sulphuretted hydrogen:—
what causes so many ill. Our chief

cure is mercury, which when taken rains
sweat upon the skin. I am unwell. Yellow plague
on us all, ague, the Amistads gone astray, this place
bog, desperate, despite its Boom River name.

I have come down with *the intermittents.*
Most have left the mission,—gone to Mercy
or to grog—so shall I. Failed? Glory be
to God; to mine [is] the failure,—better, best

if the fever had carried me off
than this
              English ship, its waves which mock.

Raymond

Diary of His Final Days with Yellow Fever

Our firstborn went. Our next dead within days
of birth, and my [wife] Eliza suffering delusions—
chills, persecution, spells. The children
are the only of the Mendi to have stayed

true to God's call:—Margru [Sarah] has done
well; Kale is too lightly clad, but still prays.
Teme and Kene [Maria and Charlotte],—none
give evidence of being Christian. Eliza says

she sees Margru always about to enslave
her. I want to find us higher ground:—a roof
without rats, a dry mission. My share I have
killed of vermin. I am sick of swamp, of trades,—

Lord, forgive!—in tobacco to cool Chief Tucker's heart.
[Days later R. died, in Freetown, from *the black vomit.*]

Anon

Sampler Found at the Abandoned Mission,
Sewn in an Unknown Hand

Under what Star
Are We led here

Every day Death
comes for thee
Be prepared
Bend thy knee

Jonah's whale
his Faith fed
The Dove found the Tree
after the Flood

Jesus is
the lengthening Chain
May His Light
burn you Again——

Thompson

Progress Report on the New Mission,
Hereafter Known as Mo Tappan

We have at last broken new, holy ground
And put up the walls. I have weeded out
Those sinners who Mr. Raymond,—bless his heart—
Out of fear, or high fever, had kept about:—

First, Lewis [Kin-na], who is a base hypocrite
And a vile, licentious man, having many wives all
About the country; worse than the heathen, of great
Trouble to us, he has been excommunicated and will

No longer harm. Tamar Wilson, the negress
Who helped found the first mission,—whose husband
Long since returned to New York—I recently found
Knocking about Freetown. Though to some a seamstress

—I brought her back for this purpose, to teach
And to cook,—*she has done but little except lounge*
On her sofa, and eat—too lazy to try and cure
Her sores by keeping herself clean. Unwashed

And unwanted, she was cast out. Christian charity
Allowed me to take in wool-headed James Covey
Who believed he was bewitched,—he was quick
Cured of that. Repented:—yet was taken soon sick

And died. He is the first to be buried in the dry
Ground here. Near, the children learn Geography
With Maps, Scriptures, Writing in Copy-Books,
Writing on Slates, and Needlework,—

Loyal as dogs to work and the Word.
Tappan, who names our place, would be proud
Indeed. I only hope Sarah, stateside,
Studying, does not return to us full of pride,

Or vanity, or worldliness. I wrote her of this,
Warned:—*Look to this matter, Sarah, pray,*—
If you have been tempted to get fine dresses,
Or bonnets, give them or throw them away

But do not bring them here. I would sooner see
Fall dead on the wharf at once such a missionary.

Covey

Deathbed Confession, in Delirium,
Written in Dirt

I returned here with my soul
bedeviled, by dæmons pursued,—
at the Mission, some say Satan's will
casts such spells, but I know men
& what they can do. Dealt
like cards, made slave then a hand
on deck, of me there's little left

that needs not be blessed. Pray,
tell:—how I got here, wandered all
over creation in lands some call
heathen, me home. We die
alone, without even our old names
etched into stone. Graves
our kin,—who remains—cannot read.

[Won't.] Still, I believe there are days
my name is not unknown. Devil,
be gone! Save a prayer
for me whose words no more
fly with the wind that whirls
the dust, our world, this cyclone
outrun by no one.

Sarah

Letter from Oberlin College, Ohio,
Preparing to Voyage to the Mission

Am saddened to hear of late
poor Charlotte, *died*
without hope, as your last
letter states. I am hard

studying Roman history, algebra,
physiology, the sonnet. I dare not
to tell what [I would like] for fear
you will not get it but at any rate

I tell what it is. It is [accordion].
I know you will laugh when I tell
what it is. *You know that people*
often says that the African

likes music. I am God's instrument:—
I fear not disease, nor the Devil,—
                                        only rust!

★　★　★

Notes

John Quincy Adams (1767–1848), Harvard man, was the only U.S. President (1825–1829) to serve in Congress (1831–1848) *after* his term in the White House. In 1841 he argued successfully before the Supreme Court to free the *Amistad* rebels rather than return them to the slave traders who bought them or give them to the navy who commandeered the mutinied ship. ("Correspondance")

Antonio, Cabin Boy (as he is often called here), was spared by the Africans during the rebellion in order to translate between the Mendi and the Spaniards who bought them. Though he was often an unreliable translator and seemed to align himself with the Spaniards, he disappeared sometime during the trial rather than remain with them in slavery. ("Exodus," "Maroon")

Captain Ferrer helmed the *Amistad* through the storms that delayed it on what should have been a brief trip from Havana to Puerto Principe. He was killed with the cook in the uprising while some of the crew escaped over the side—reportedly to reach land and tell of their ordeal. ("Buzzard," "Westville")

Celestino, the Cook on the *Amistad*, was suspected of being the son of Captain Ferrer as well as his manservant. He reportedly mimed through hand gestures that the Mendi were to be killed and eaten after leaving Cuba, which may have precipitated the mutiny by the Africans as much as the worsening conditions did. ("Cut-Up," "Friendship")

Cinque (1814–1879) was a rice planter with a wife and three children before his capture and enslavement. Roughly twenty-seven years old, he led the revolt on the *Amistad,* using a nail to free himself and others on the slave ship. Upon returning to Africa in 1842, Cinque left the mission station established by the *Amistad* Committee to search for his family. Though unsuccessful, he returned to his people's customs, apparently becoming a chief among them. Disheartened missionaries heard and passed along unfounded rumors that Cinque had reverted to "paganism" and slave trading—or returned to the mission for a deathbed conversion. ("Advent," "Witness")

The Committee to free the Mendi was organized by well-intentioned abolitionists who not only sought to free the Africans but to proselytize them to Christianity. This organization, still in existence under another name, also began the mission that returned the Amistads to Mendi. Within a short time the mission failed; the Africans abandoned it, presumably to find their families. ("Broadway," "After Word")

James Covey, translator for the captured Mendi, was discovered on the docks by one of the abolitionists who searched for a native speaker by counting to ten in Mendi. As a young man, Covey himself had been captured and then saved by a British ship and returned to Freetown. At that time, the international slave trade was officially illegal (though one could still be born into chattel slavery, a loophole particular to the Americas); of course, unofficially the trade was sanctioned if not by law then by action and inaction. Covey speaks not as a prisoner but to and for the Mendi. ("Buzzard")

Fu-li, a fellow Mendi, was apparently branded by Captain Ferrer ("Exodus") and later converted to Christianity, even changing his name. ("Gentleman")

Kale was the youngest of the *Amistad* captives, and one of the first to learn English. Often he was asked to spell words and religious phrases to prove both the Mendi's devotion and intelligence. ("Broadway," "Westville," "Lexicon")

Kin-na was an unmarried young man when kidnapped on the War Road. ("New Haven," "After Word")

Marghu (renamed Sarah) was one of three young girls bought by one of the Spaniards—for what purpose we can only imagine. She remained faithful to the church, attending Oberlin College and returning to the mission when she graduated. ("Jubilat," "After Word")

The Spaniards Montes and Ruiz bought the Amistads, mostly Mendi, from a trader in Cuba. Because even in Cuba newly captured African slaves (*bozales*) were illegal, the men forged papers, giving the Mendi Christian and Spanish names in order to pretend they were *ladinos* born in Cuba.

Steele was one of the white missionaries sent to Sierra Leone with the Amistads in order to establish a mission. ("Soundings," "Gentleman," "After Word")

Lewis Tappan was the white abolitionist who championed the Amistads' cause. He is an important American figure, discussed at length by poet Muriel Rukeyser in her biography of Willard Gibbs. The Mendi wrote him seeking aid in their release. ("Correspondance," "After Word")

Tucker was a local leader in Sierra Leone near the original mission. Appeasing him was customary, but morally fraught for some of the missionaries. ("Gentleman," "After Word")

The Wilsons, husband and wife, were African American missionaries who accompanied the Amistads on their return, in order to set up the mission. Their fate is hard to surmise, though they were soon separated, with Mr. Wilson returning to the United States. Tamar Wilson apparently returned to the mission. ("After Word")

★

For this chronicle, I have relied on several historical sources. John Wesley Blassingame's *Slave Testimony* proved crucial, providing the Mendi's actual letters that started my writing what would become the poems of the Correspondance section. Many other so-called history texts were thin on footnotes and heavy on fiction—the latter in and of itself not a problem, except that the slant was always obvious and, most often, troubling. Generally speaking, I have sought to avoid other fictional or poetic versions of the events. Nevertheless, I would be remiss if I did not mention William Owens's *Slave Mutiny* (renamed *Black Mutiny* in the 1960s) which provided useful texture and occasional background along the way.

Two historically reliable texts were Mary Cable's *Black Odyssey,* especially useful for my "After Word" (where italics are actual quotes from their speakers); and the fine account provided by Muriel Rukeyser in her biography of Willard Gibbs—the very one that influenced Robert Hayden's classic poem "Middle Passage." Remarkably balanced and fascinating is John Warner Barber's original 1840 account, *A History of the Amistad Captives,* which provided the illustrations for this book.

In the end, I hope this is as much the Mendi's, and Merica's, as mine.

—K.L.Y.

A NOTE ABOUT THE AUTHOR

Kevin Young is the author of six previous books of poetry, including *Dear Darkness,* winner of the Southern Independent Bookseller's Award in poetry, and *Jelly Roll: A Blues,* a finalist for the National Book Award and the *Los Angeles Times* Book Prize, and winner of the Paterson Poetry Prize. Young is also editor of five other volumes, including Library of America's *John Berryman: Selected Poems* and Everyman's Library Pocket Poet anthologies *Blues Poems* and *Jazz Poems.* His most recent anthology *The Art of Losing: Poems of Grief and Healing* appeared in March 2010; his book *The Grey Album* won the 2010 Graywolf Nonfiction Prize and is forthcoming in 2012. Recently named the United States Artists James Baldwin Fellow, Young is Atticus Haygood Professor of Creative Writing and English and curator of Literary Collections and the Raymond Danowski Poetry Library at Emory University.

A NOTE ABOUT THE TYPE

⹀ This book was set in Baskerville, a facsimile of the type cast
from the original matrices designed by John Baskerville.
The original face was the forerunner of the modern group of
typefaces.

John Baskerville (1706–1775) of Birmingham, England,
was a writing master with a special renown for cutting
inscriptions in stone. About 1750 he began experimenting
with punch cutting and making typographical material, and
in 1757 he published his first work, a Virgil in royal quarto.
His types, at first criticized as unnecessarily slender, deli-
cate, and feminine, in time were recognized as both distinct
and elegant, and his types as well as his printing were
greatly admired.

Four years after his death, Baskerville's widow sold all his
punches and matrices to the Société Philosophique, Lit-
téraire et Typographique, which used some of the types for
the sumptuous Kehl edition of Voltaire's works in seventy
volumes. Eventually the punches and matrices came into
the possession of the distinguished Paris typefounders
Deberny & Peignot, who, in singularly generous fashion,
returned them to Cambridge University Press in 1953.

Composed by North Market Street Graphics,
Lancaster, Pennsylvania
Printed and bound by Berryville Graphics,
Berryville, Virgina
Designed by Virginia Tan